Beach Noise
Photography

Joseph Fleming

Decades of being around accomplished talent producing absolutely phenomenal quality work has taught that we are capable of greatness. It is possible to meet our destiny and become it. Experiencing excellence done with such apparent ease and humble selfless gratification is the motivation for my photography.

Being colorblind gives an advantage when composing black & white... less confusion. This special collection selected from thousands of captures. All images were framed in the camera and presented without edits, genuine as seen through the lens. RAW conversion applied by proprietary panchromatic process. Limited fine art prints available from original files.

Joseph Fleming

BeachNoise.com

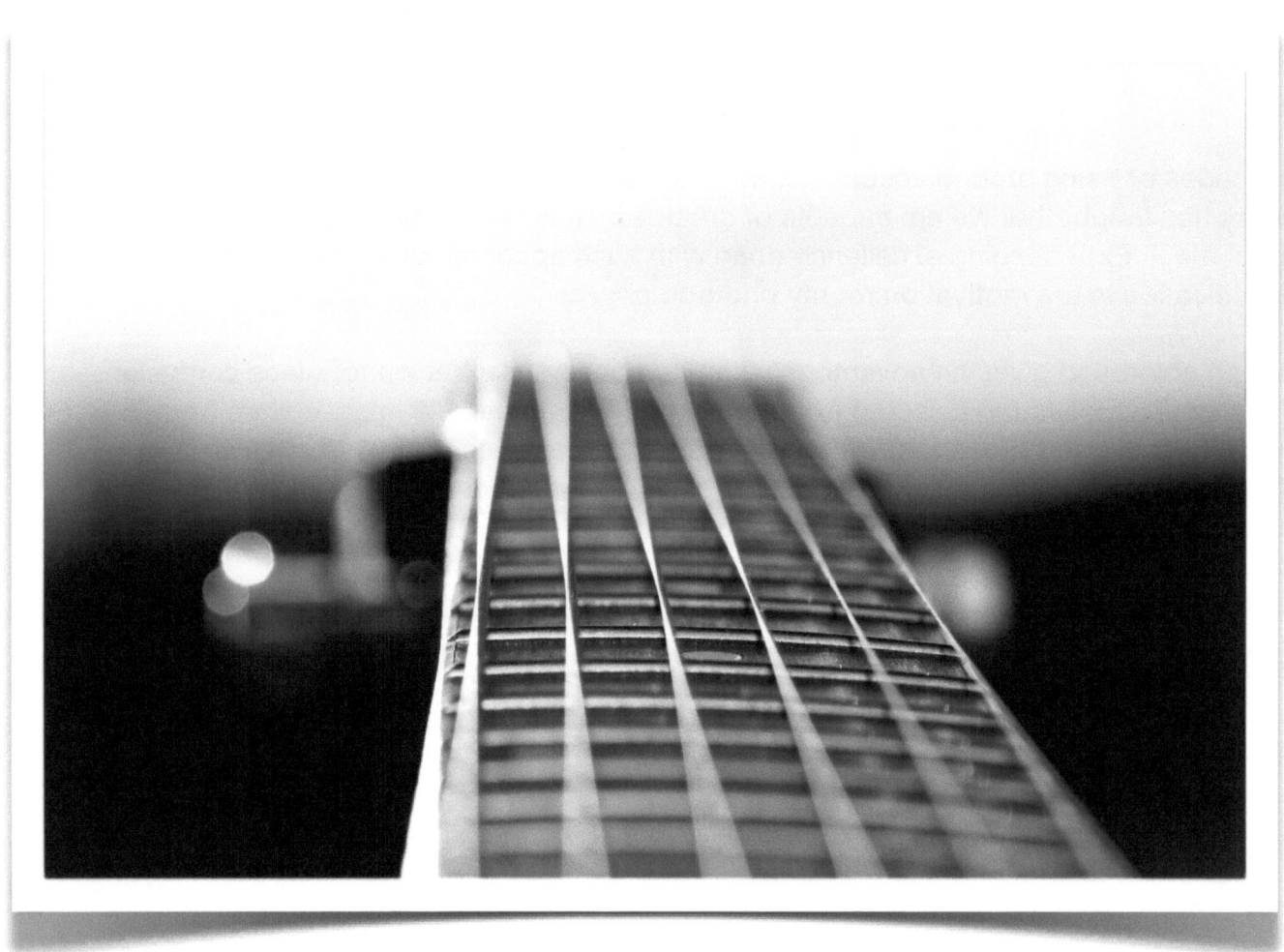

0351

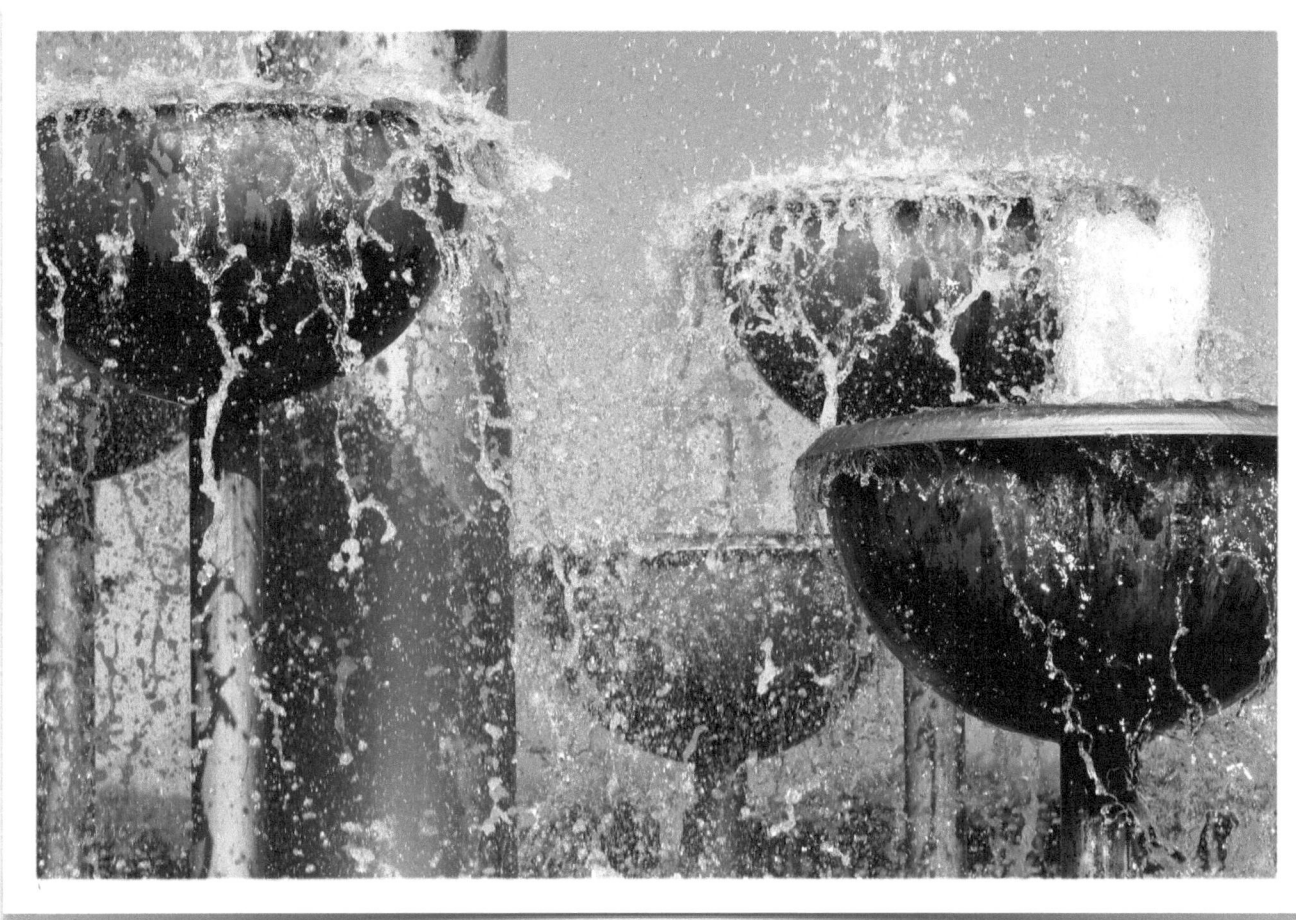

0354

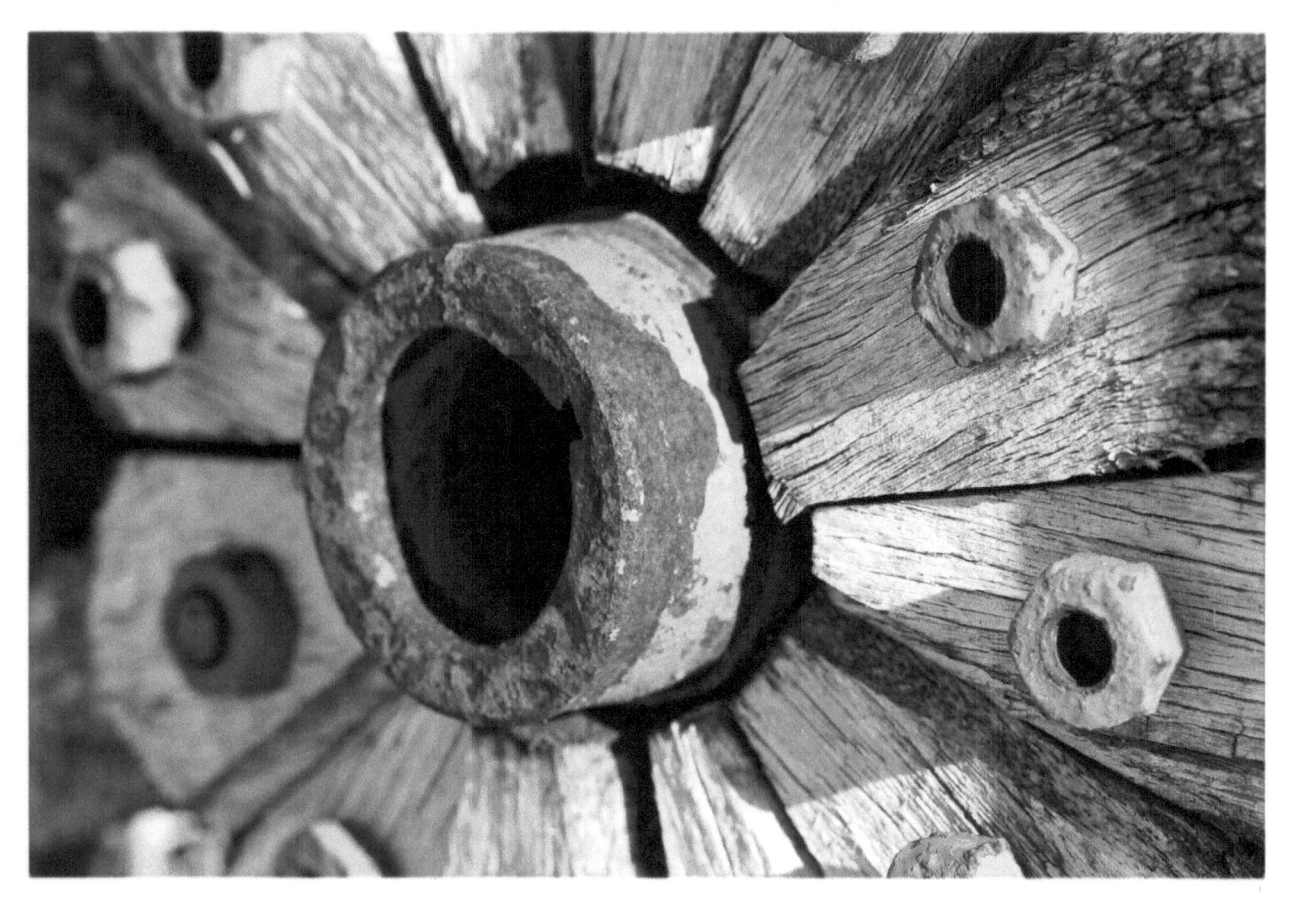

0437

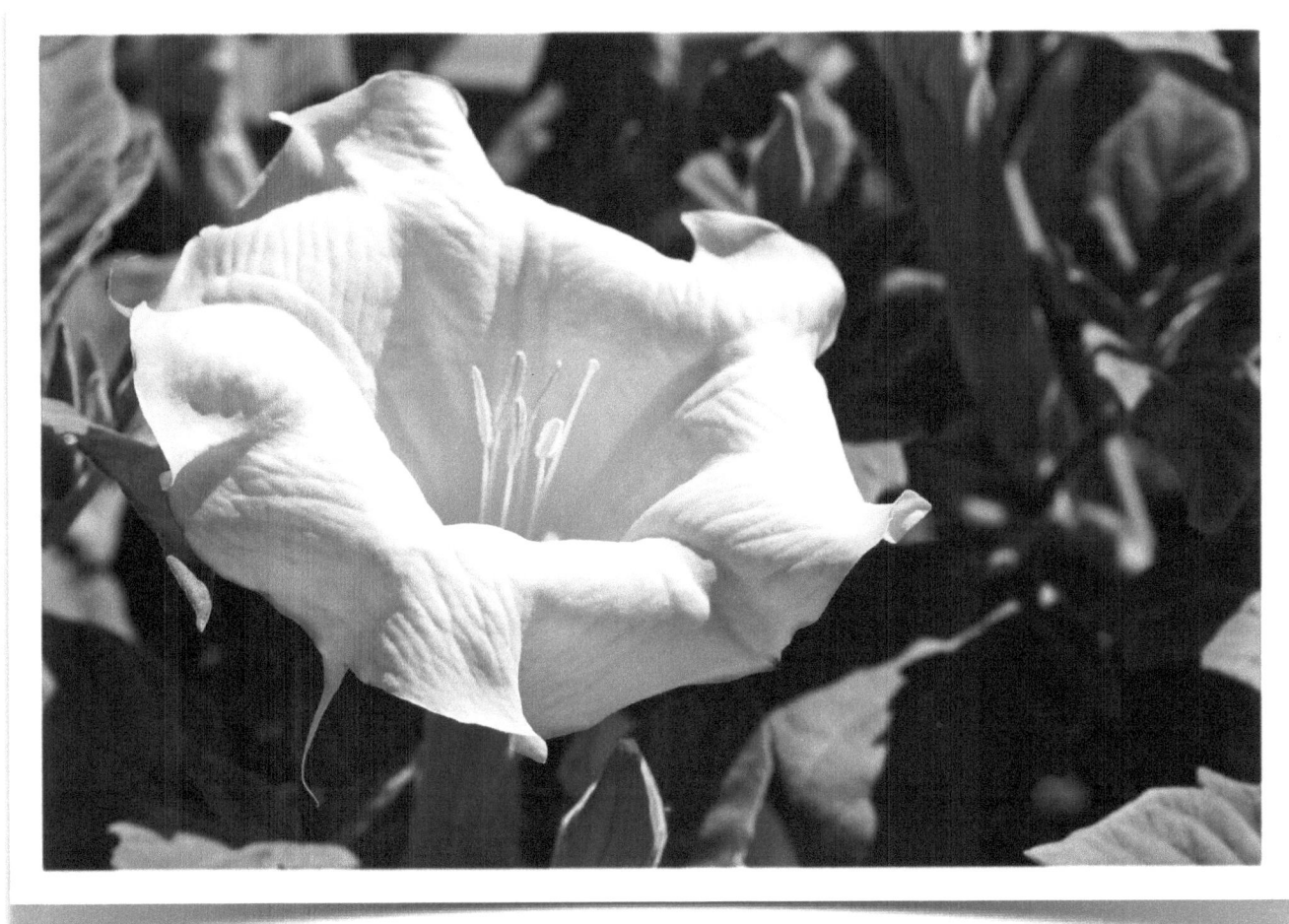

0464

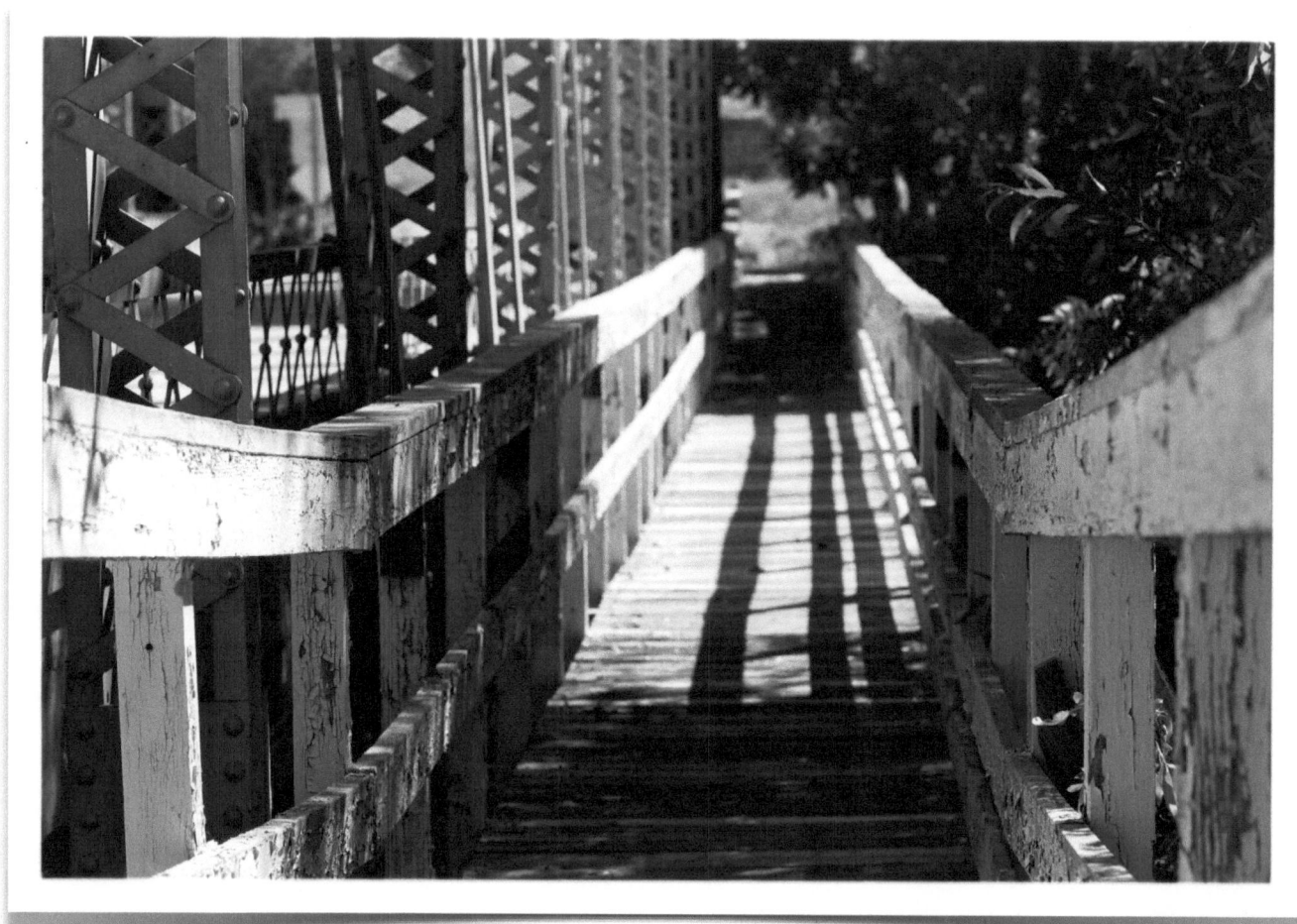

0503

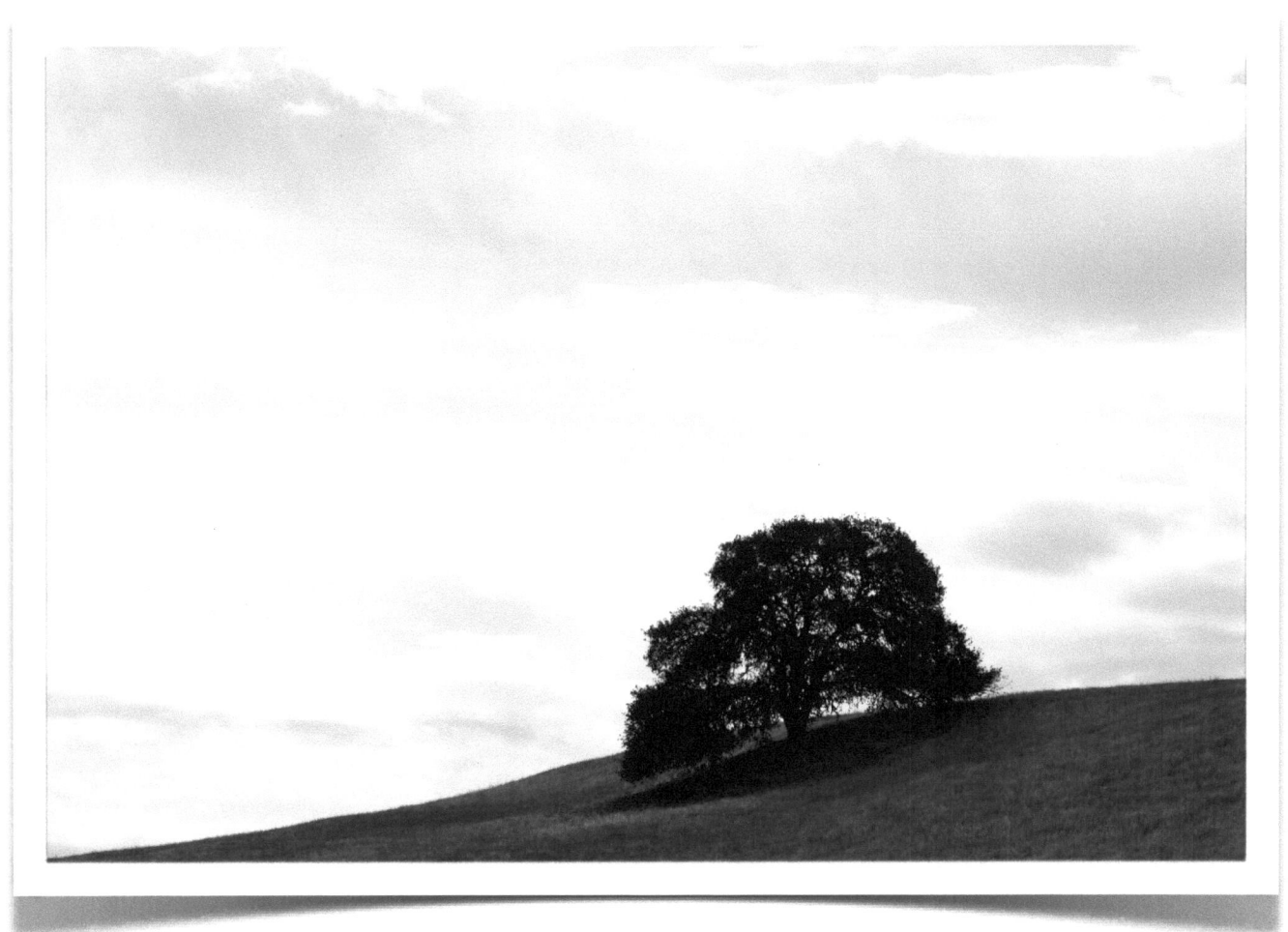

0531

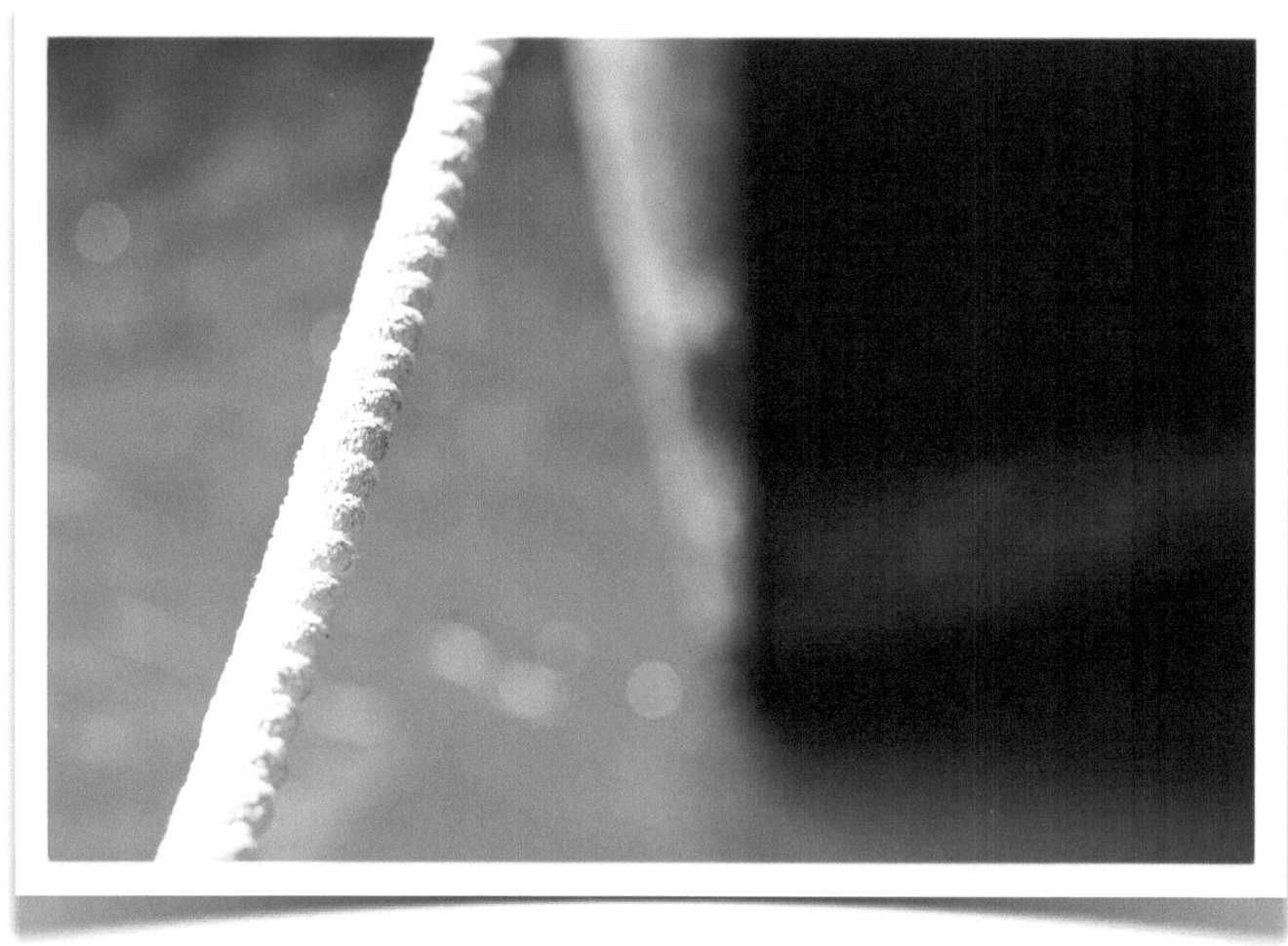

0667

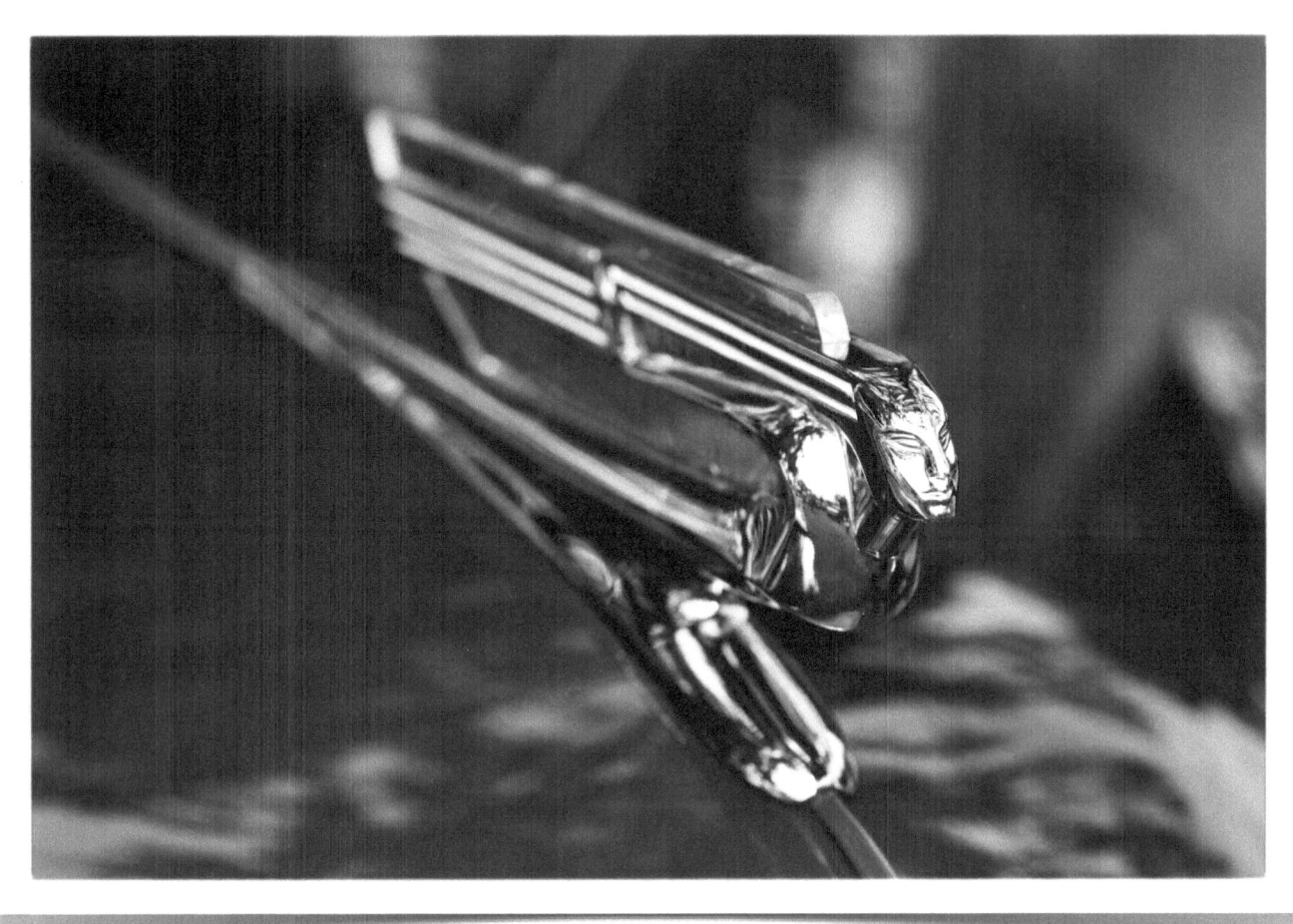

0705

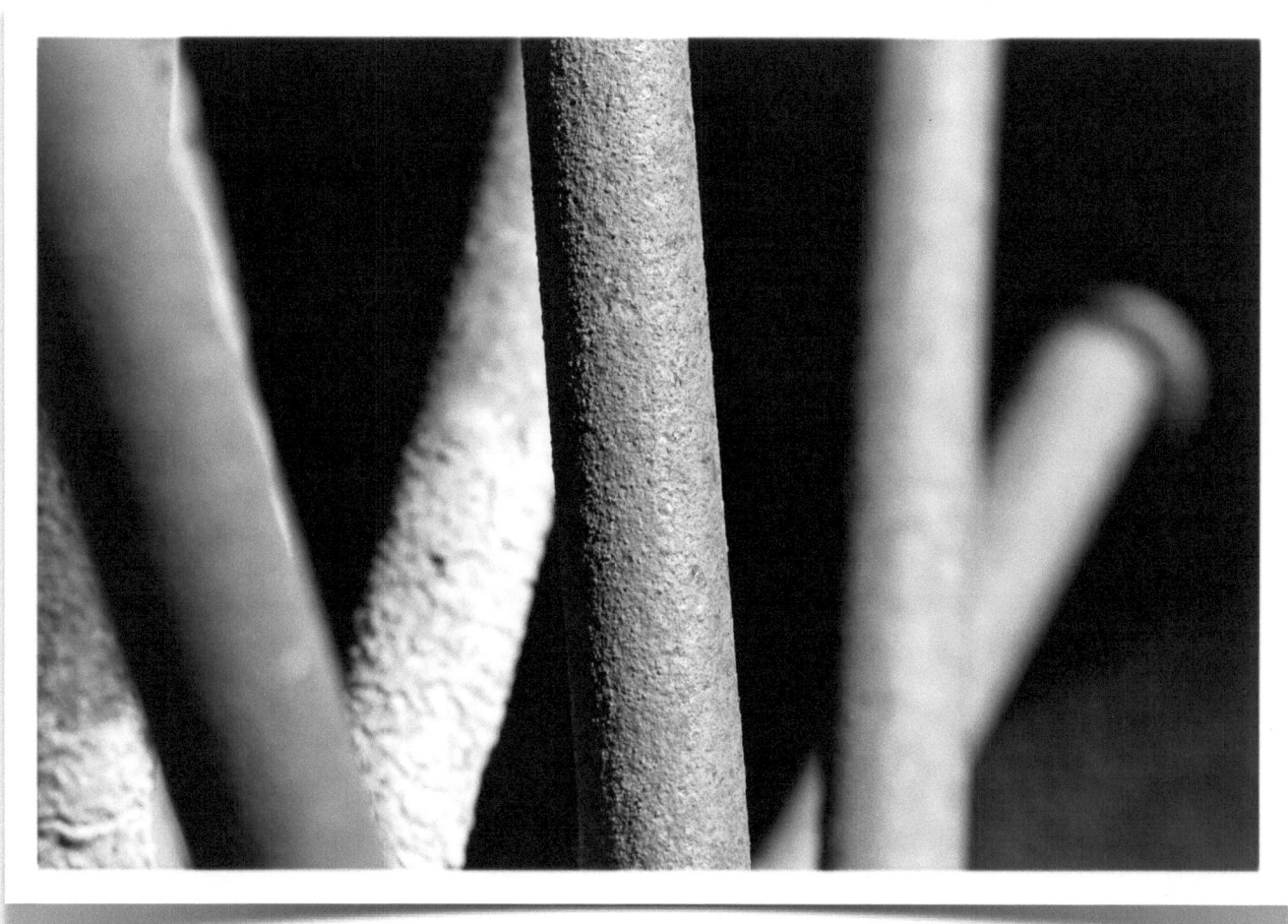

0780

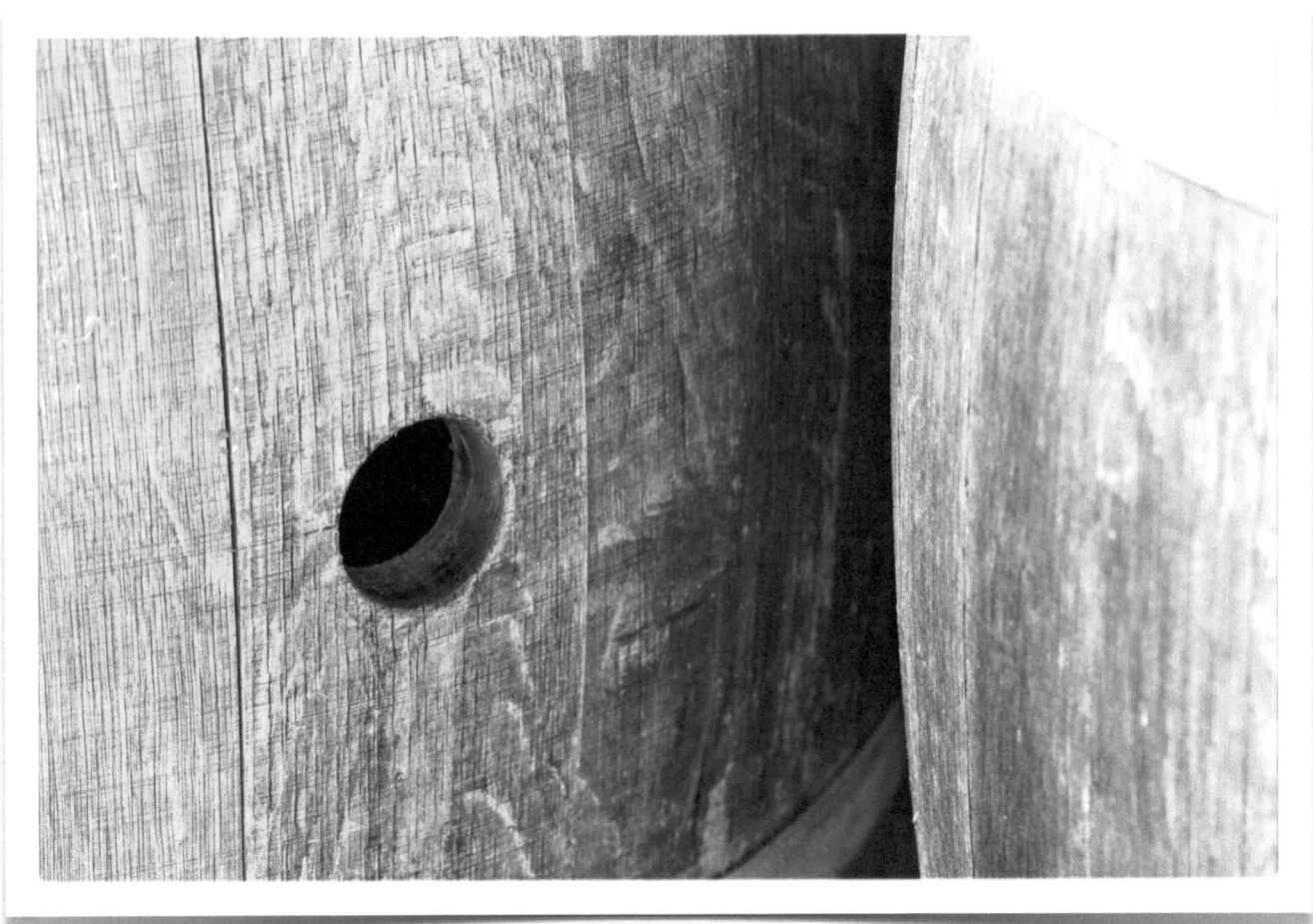

0826

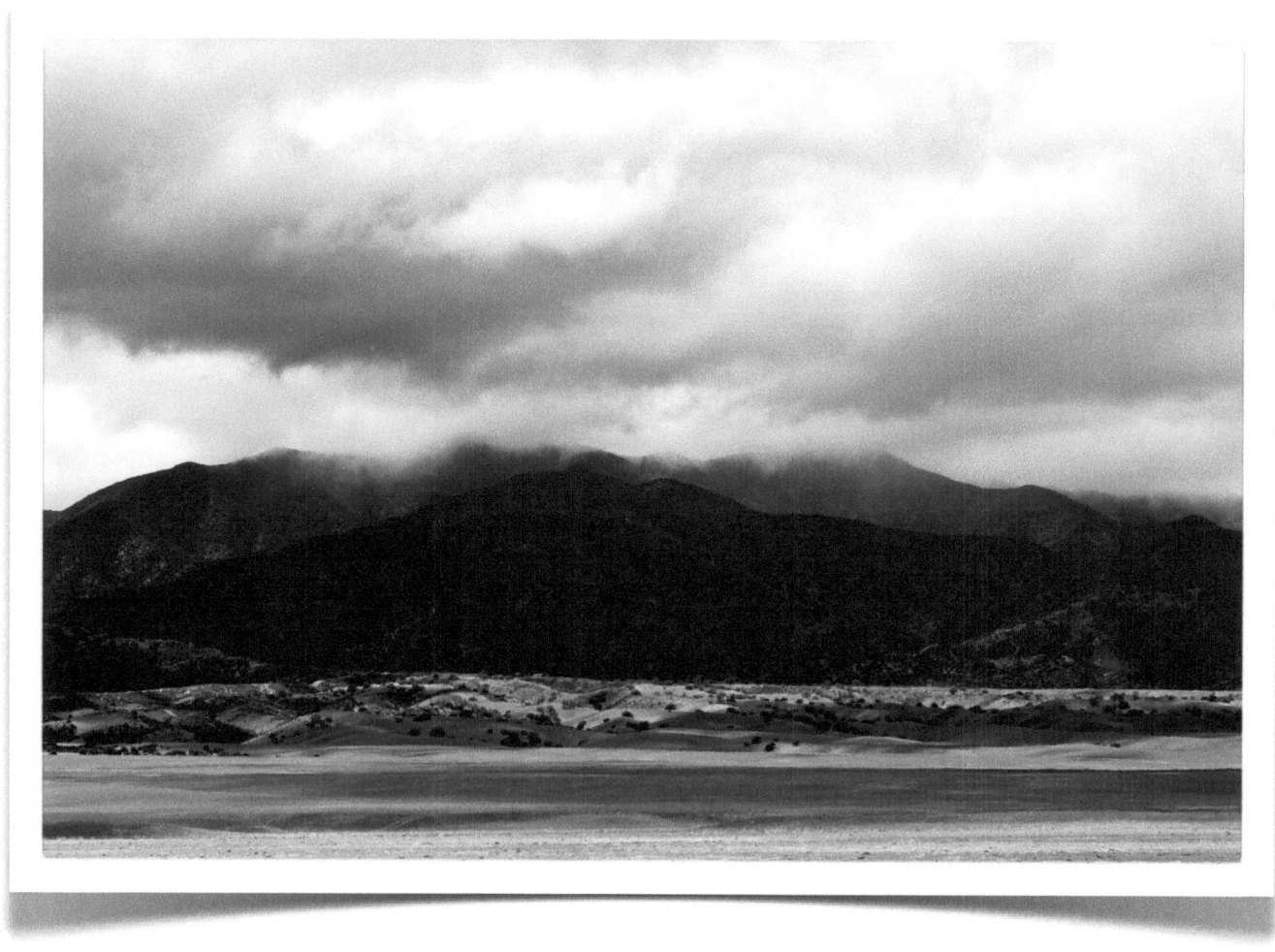

0843

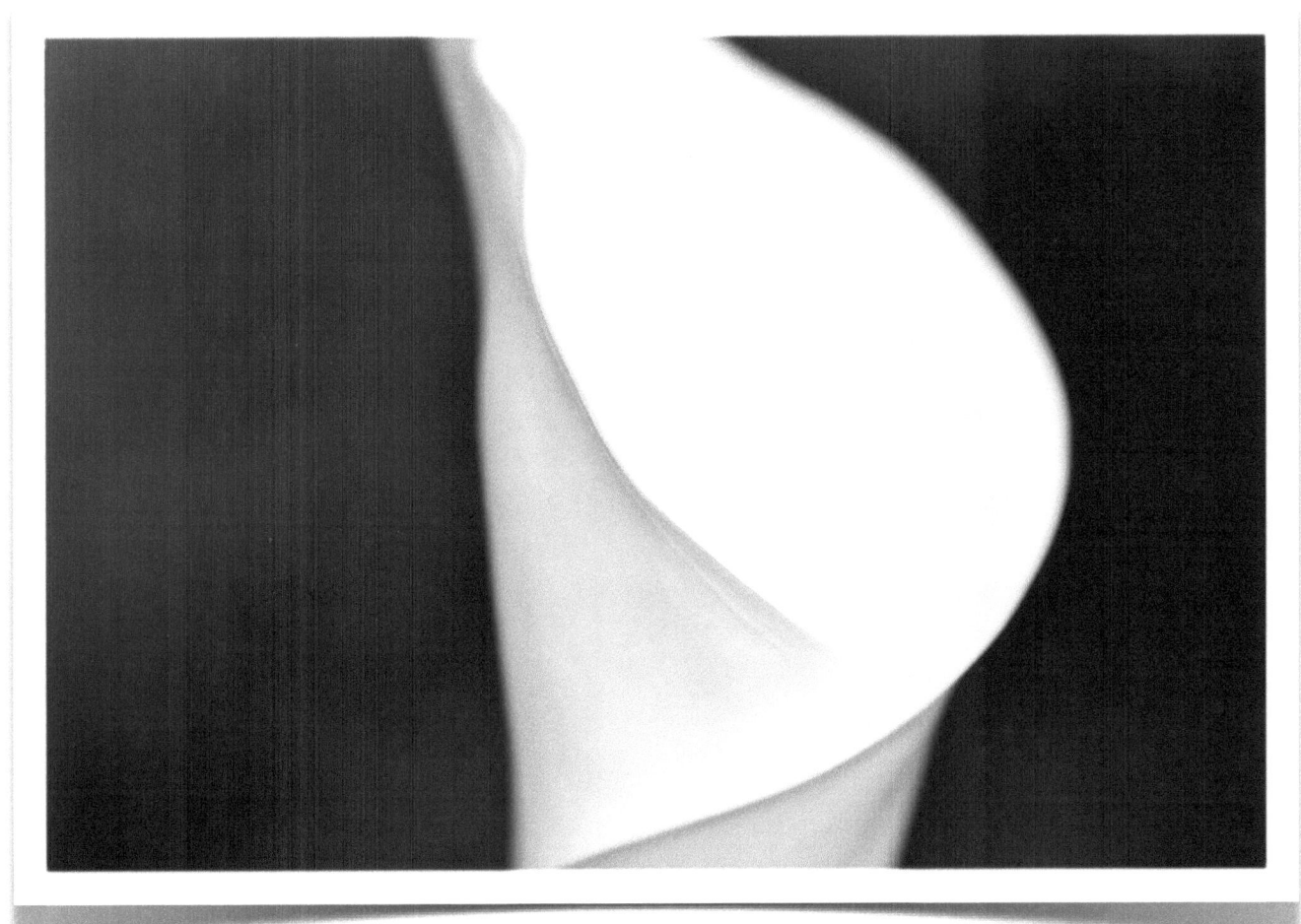

0920

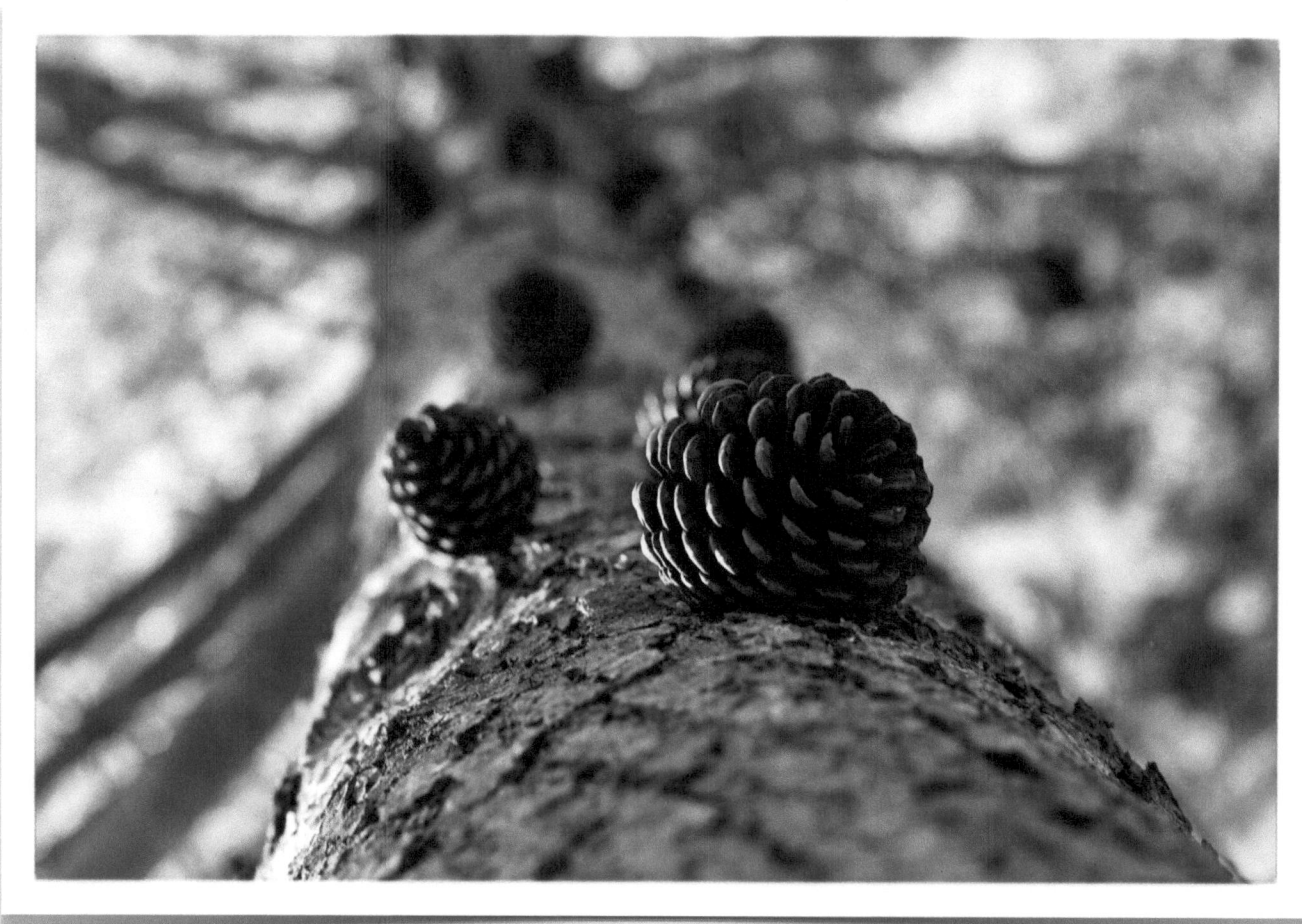

0938

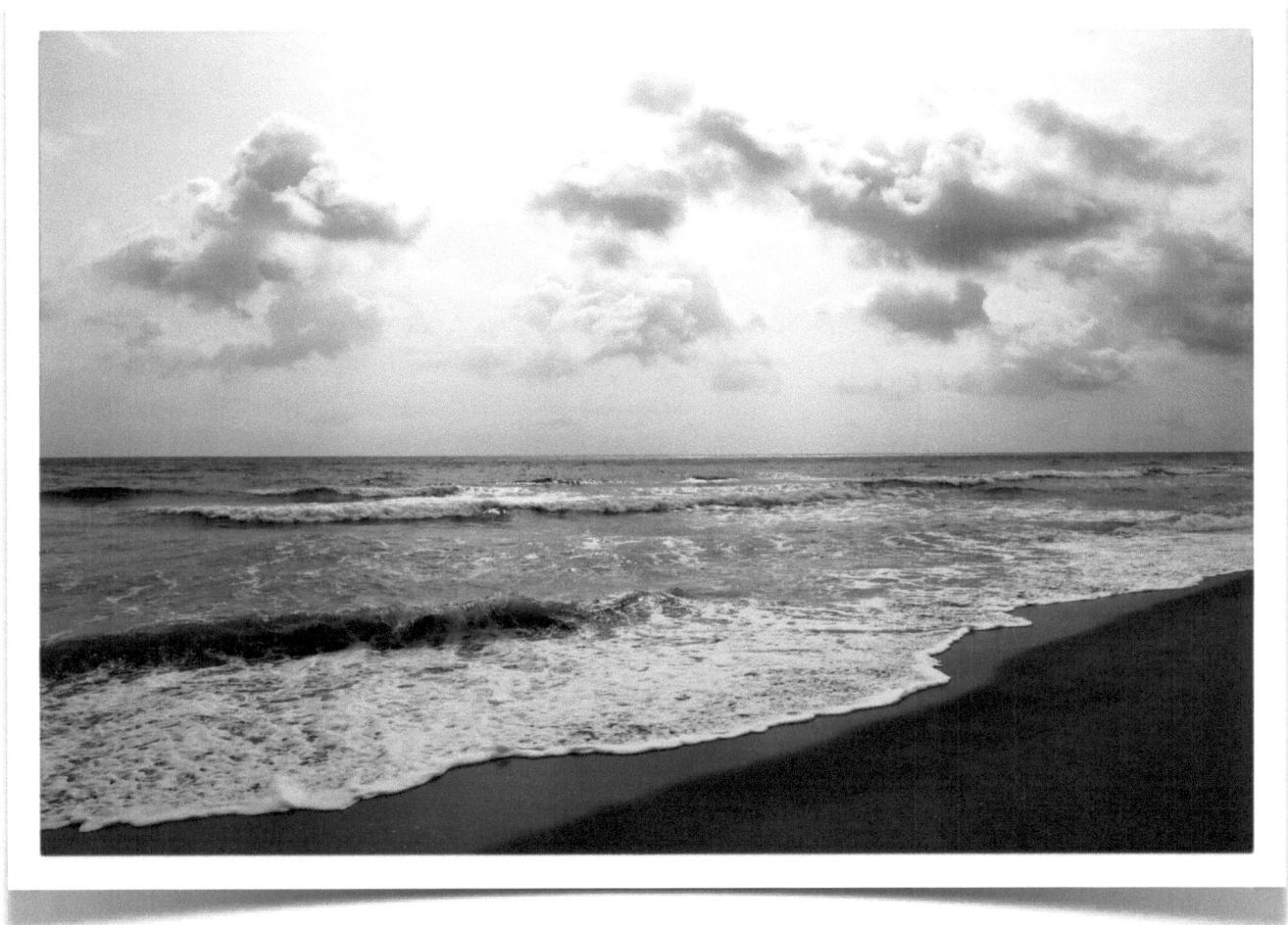

0975

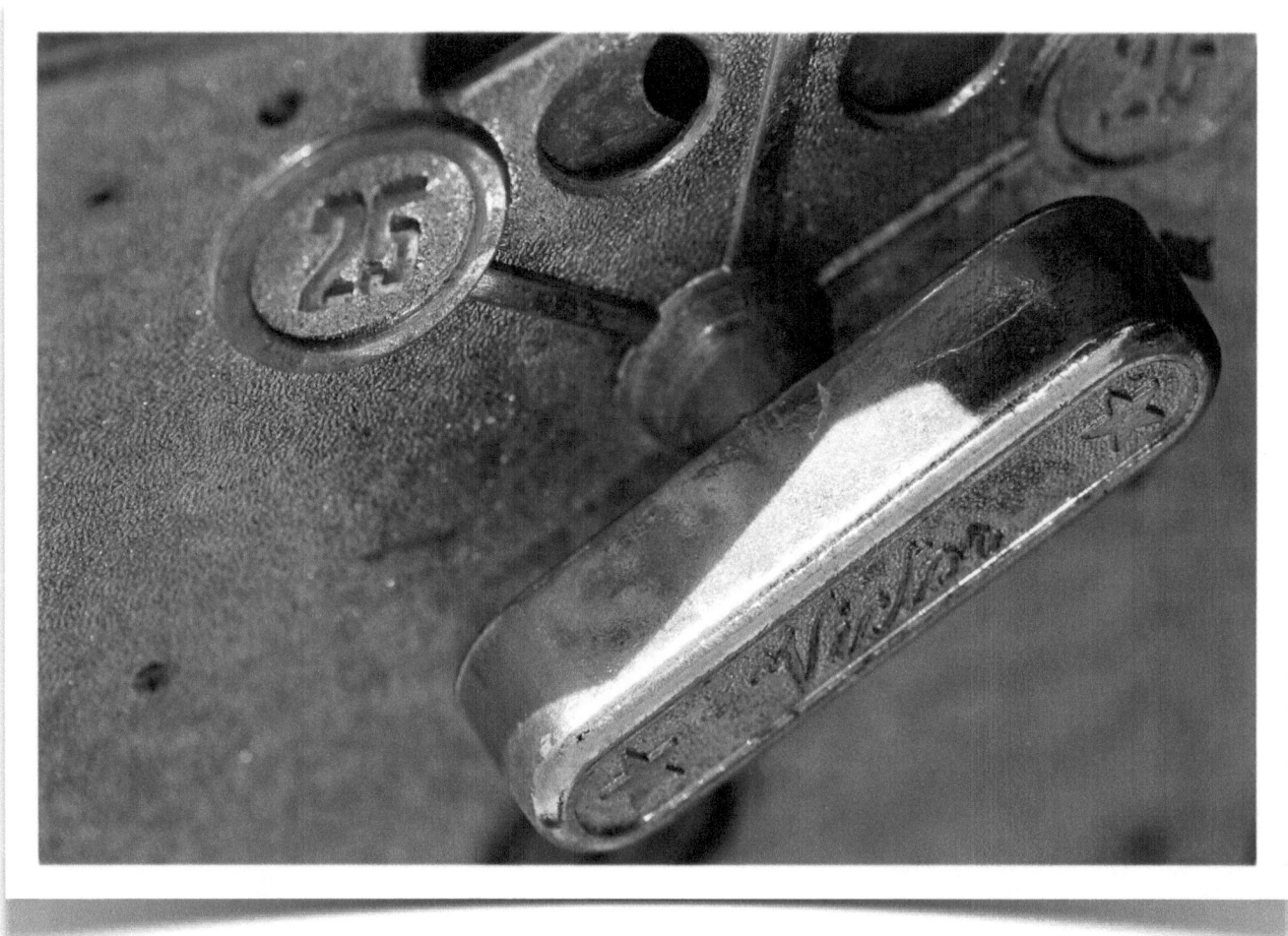

1085

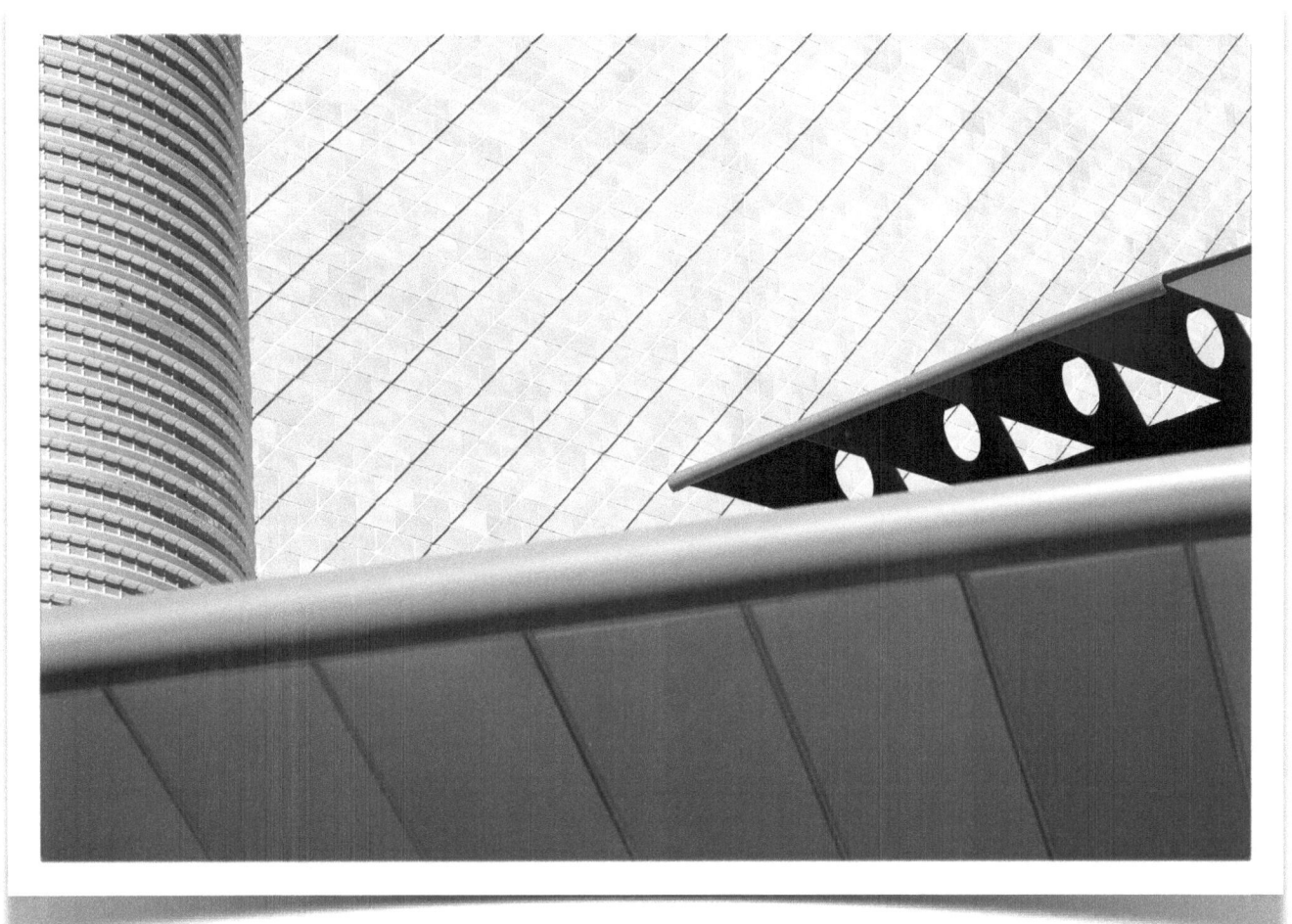

1088

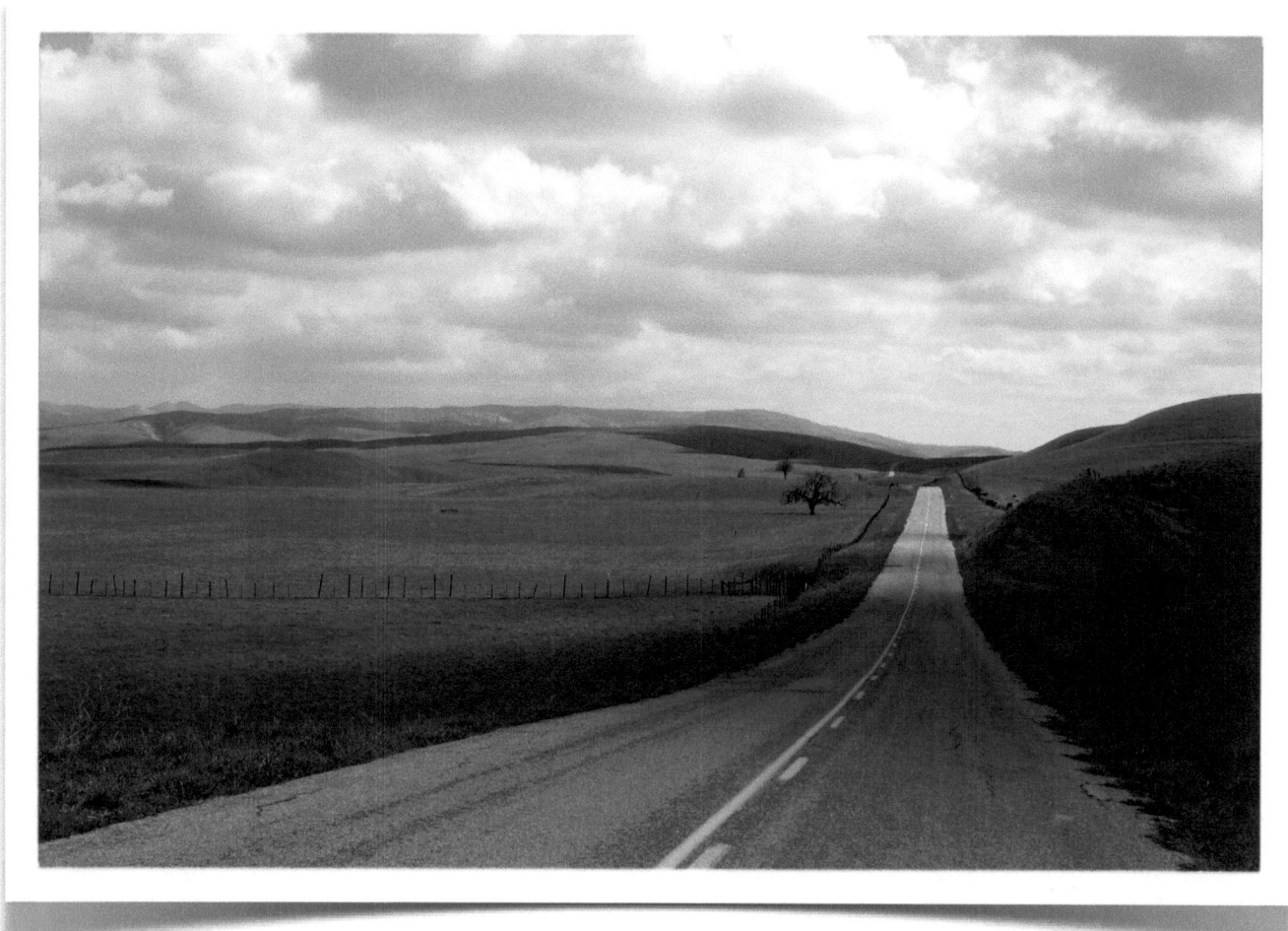

1784

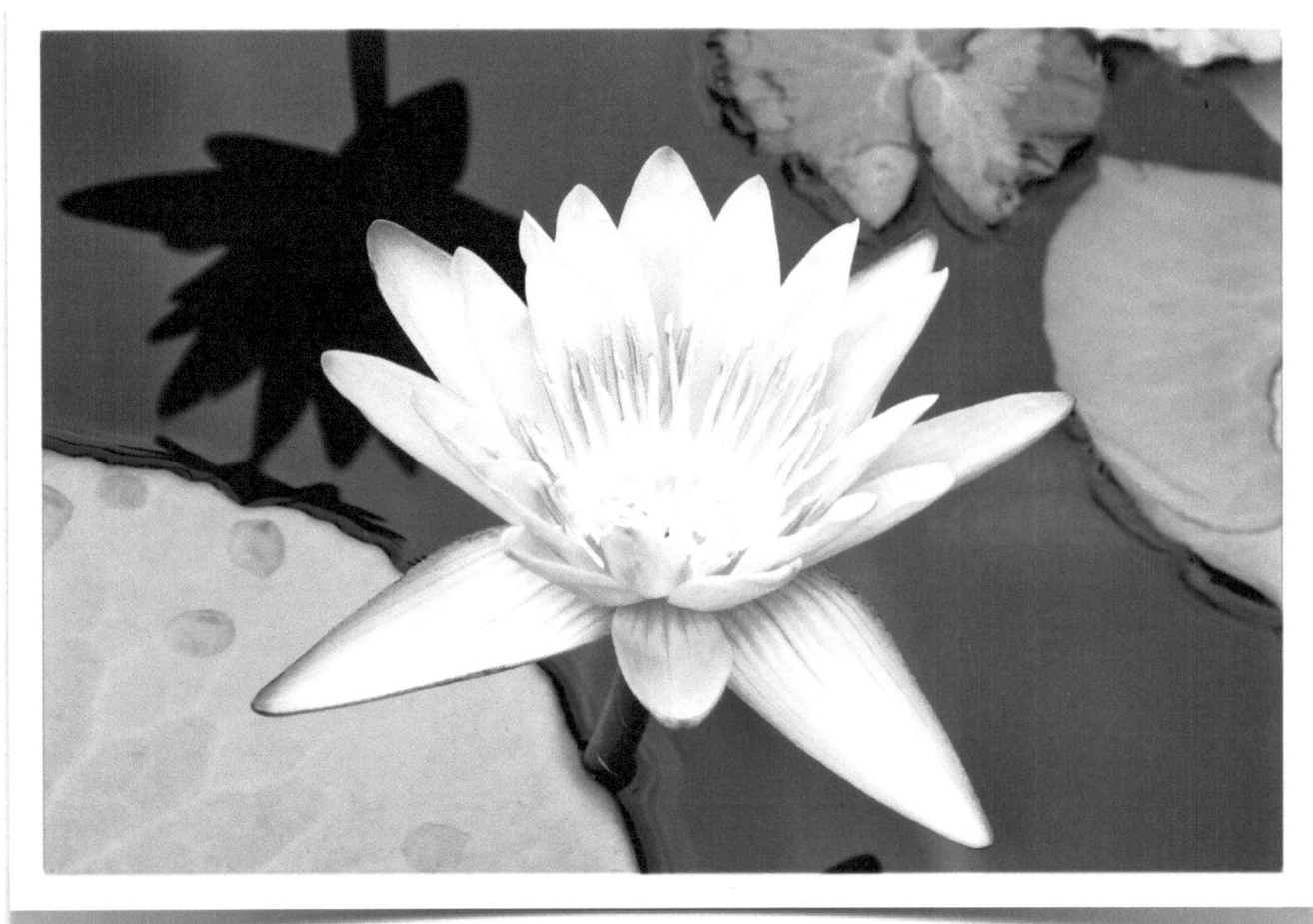

2042

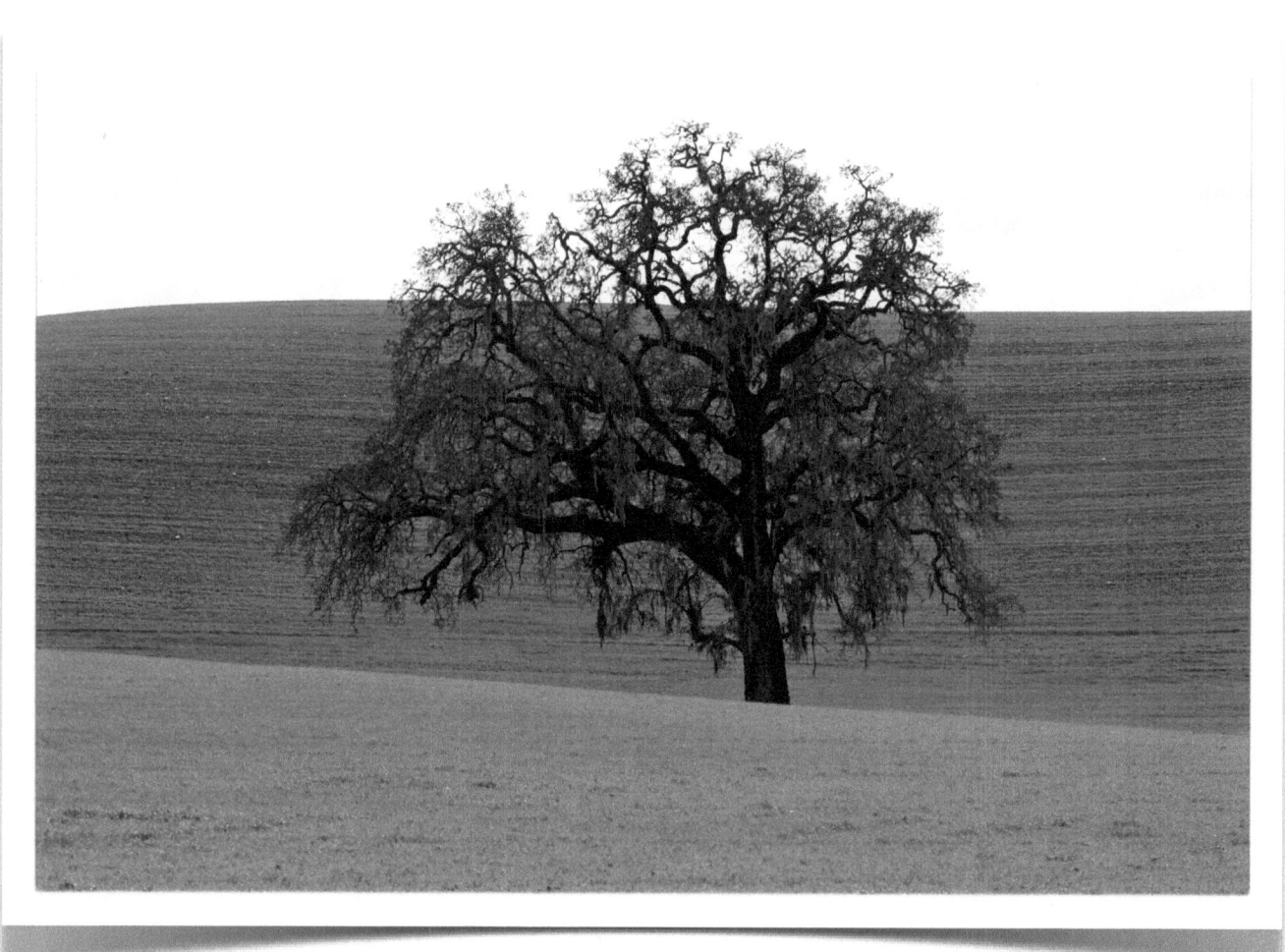

2083

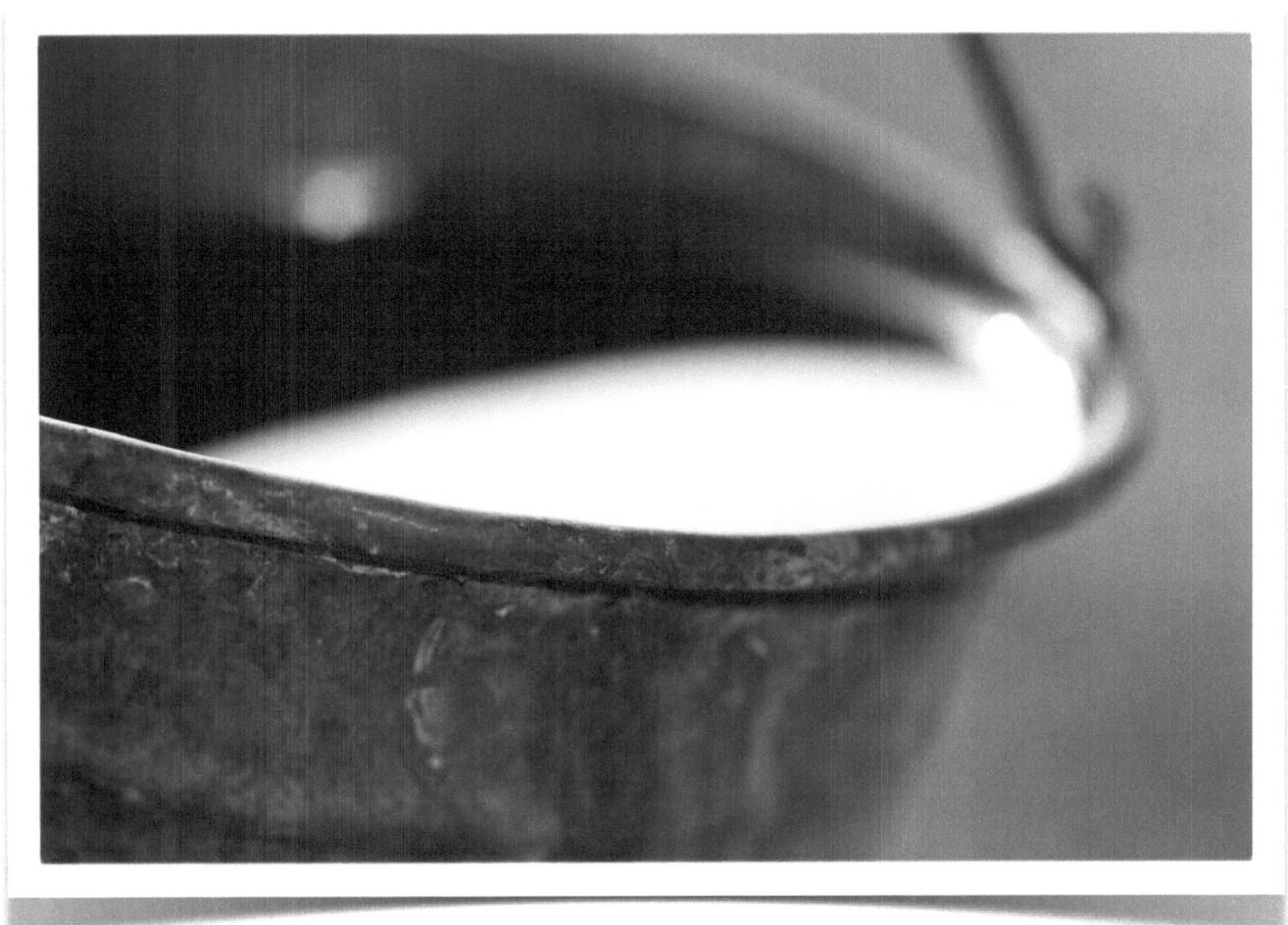

2180

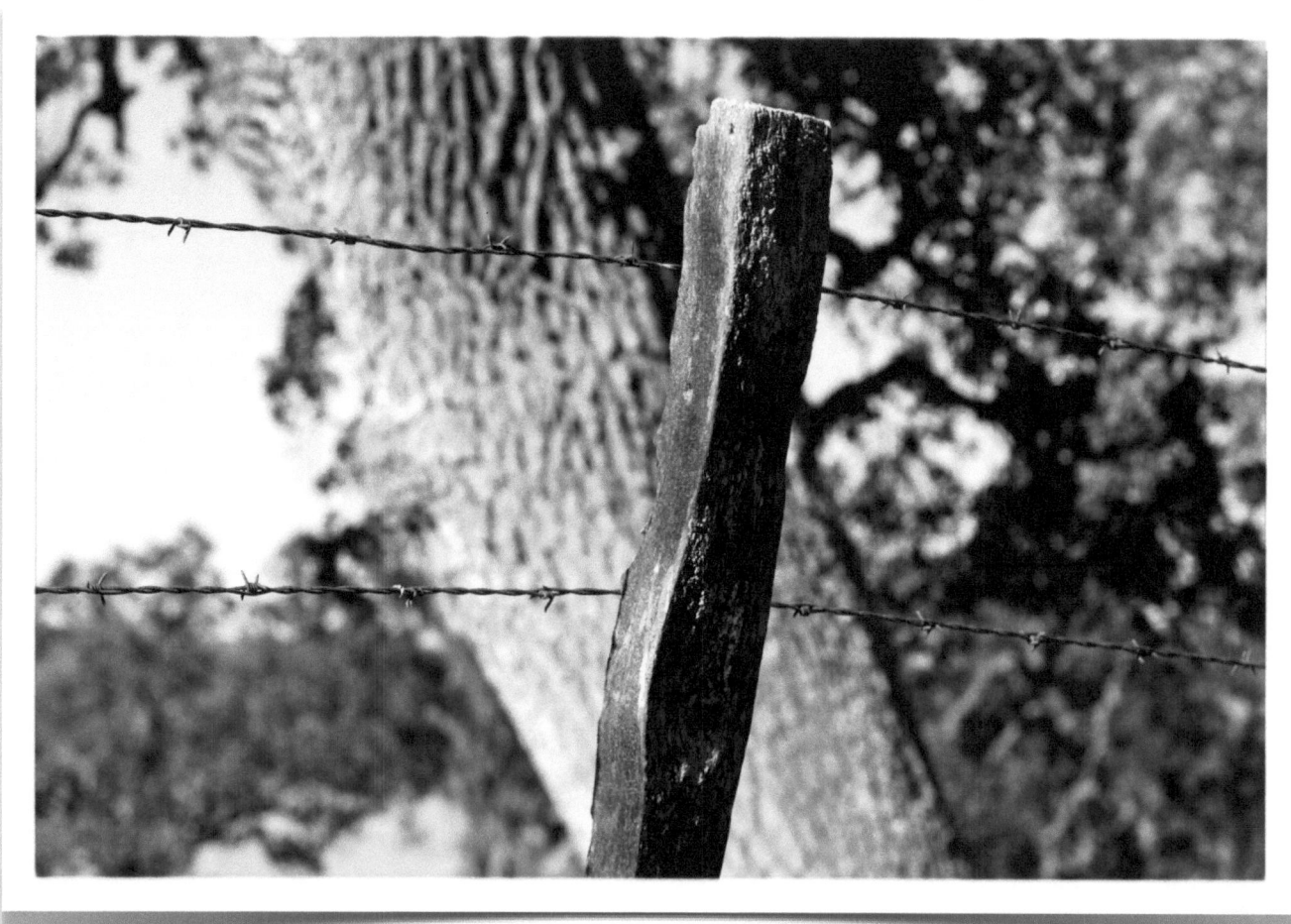

2374

2397

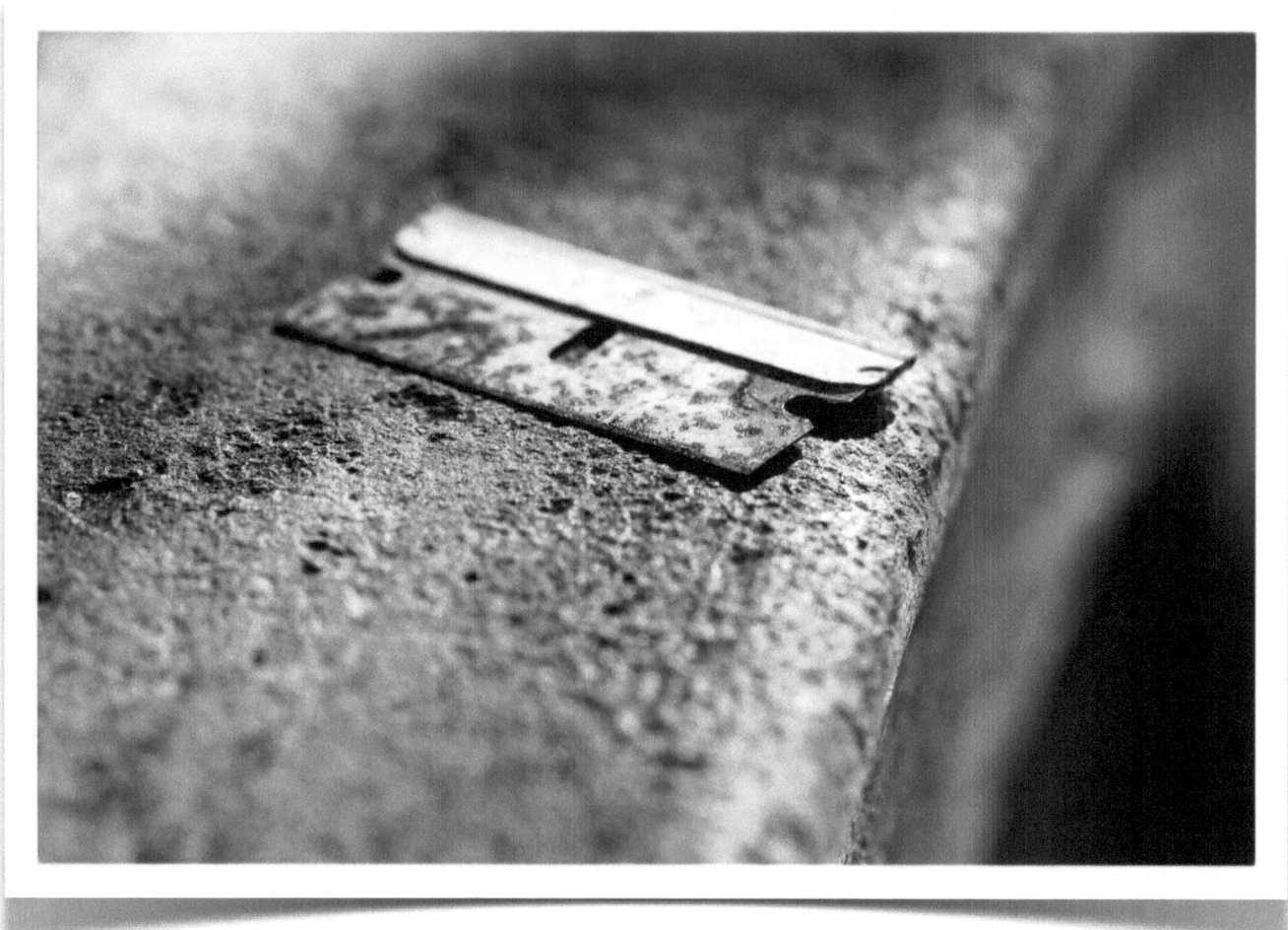

2467

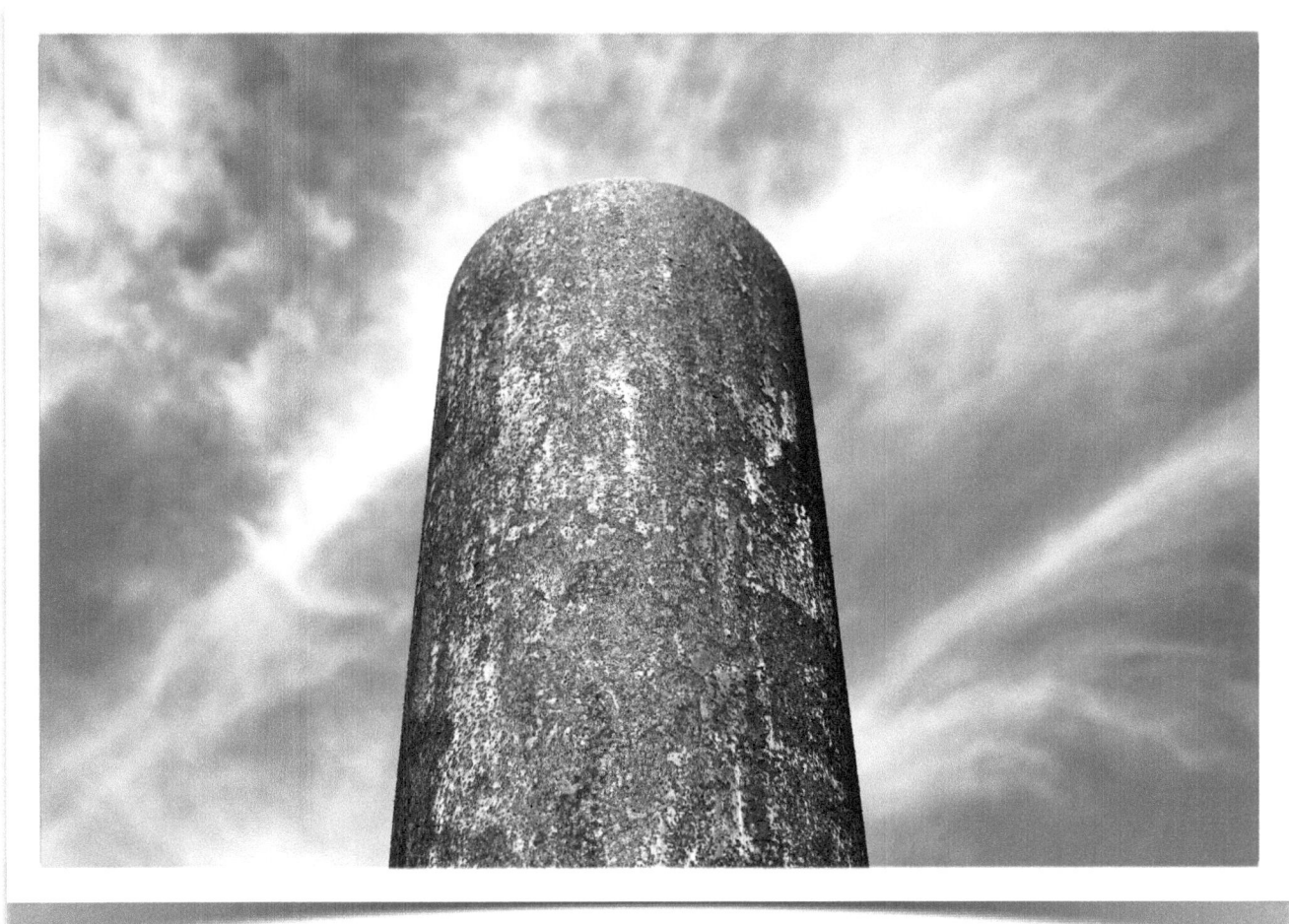

2495

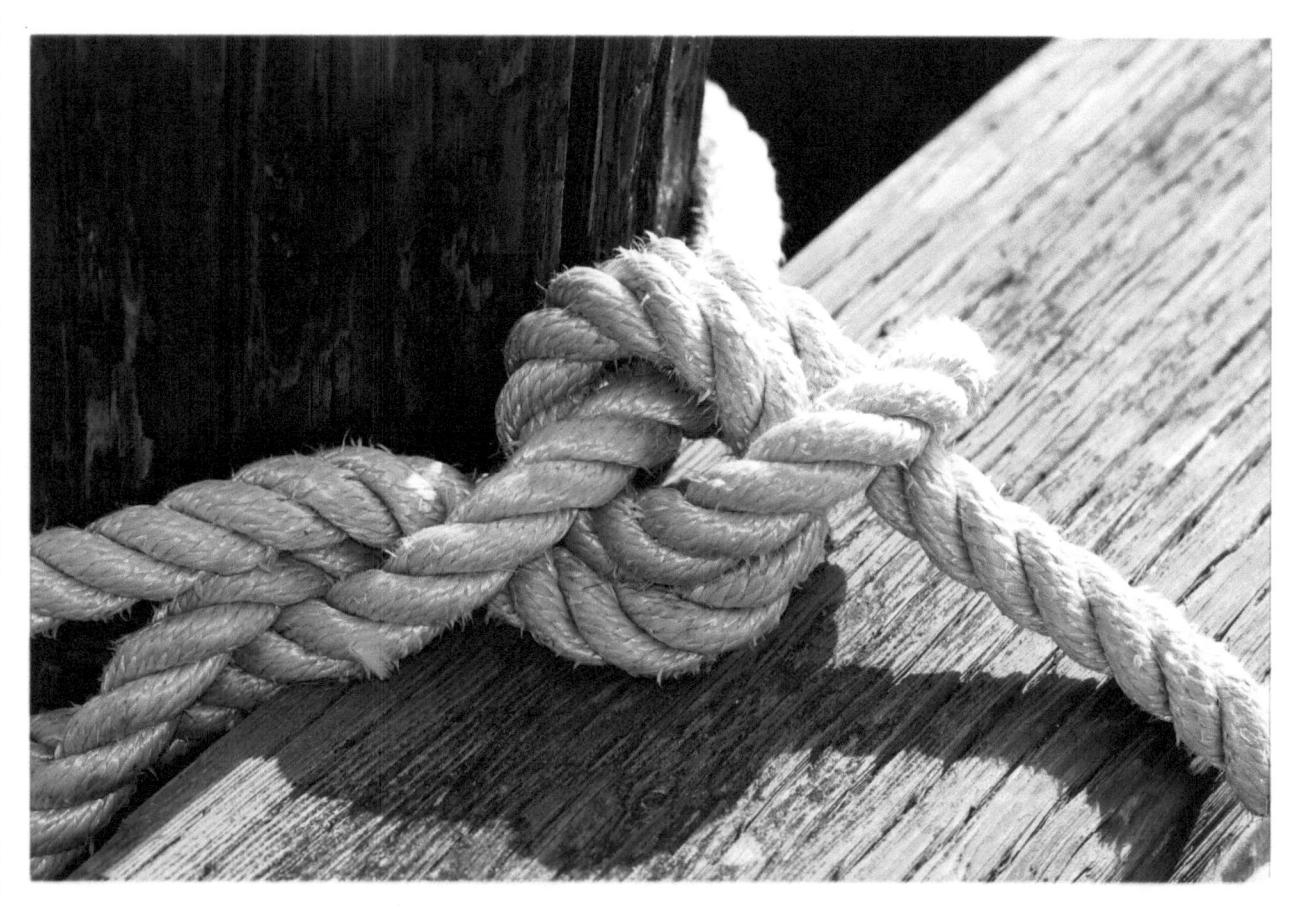

2631

2929

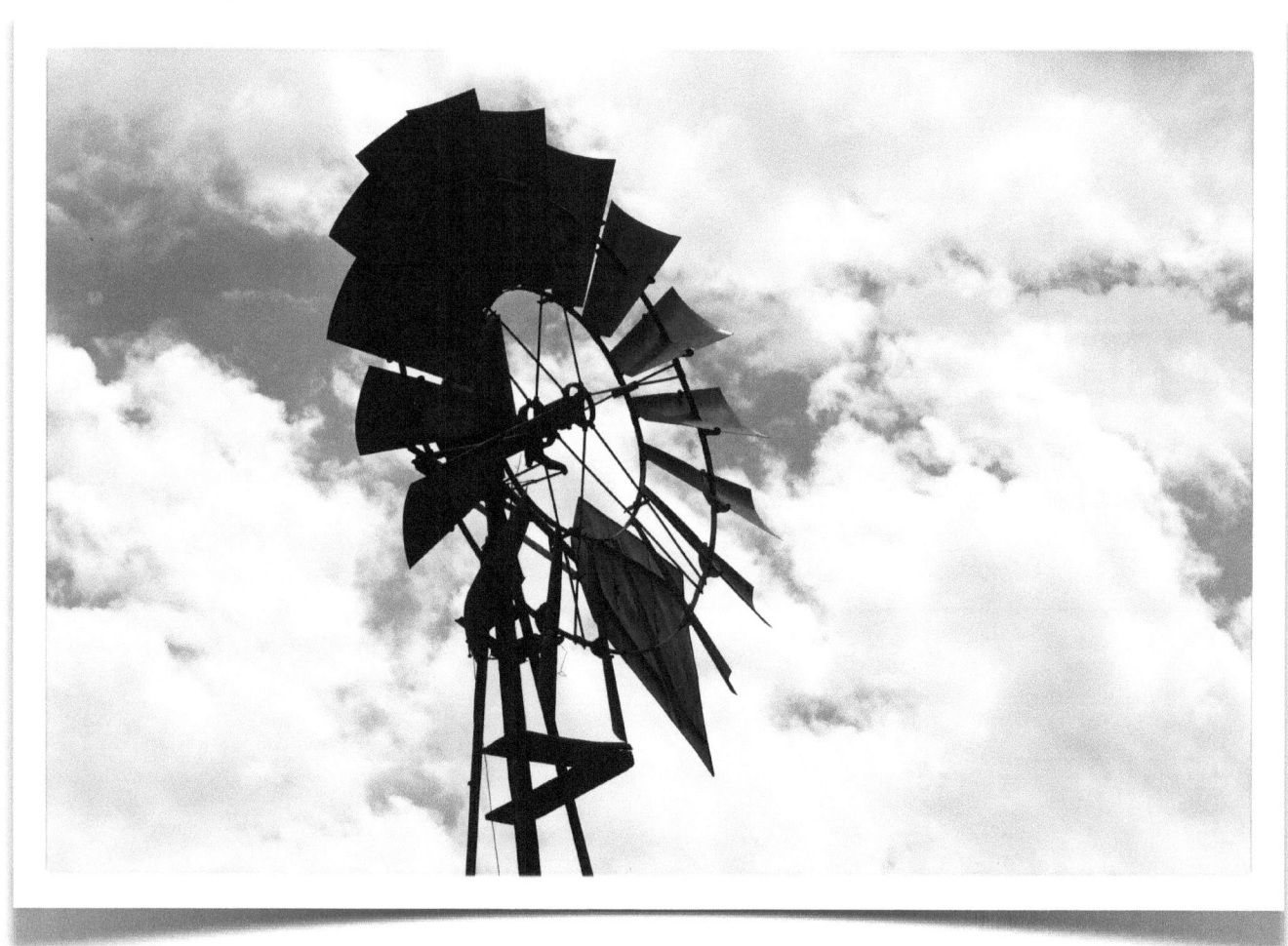

2969

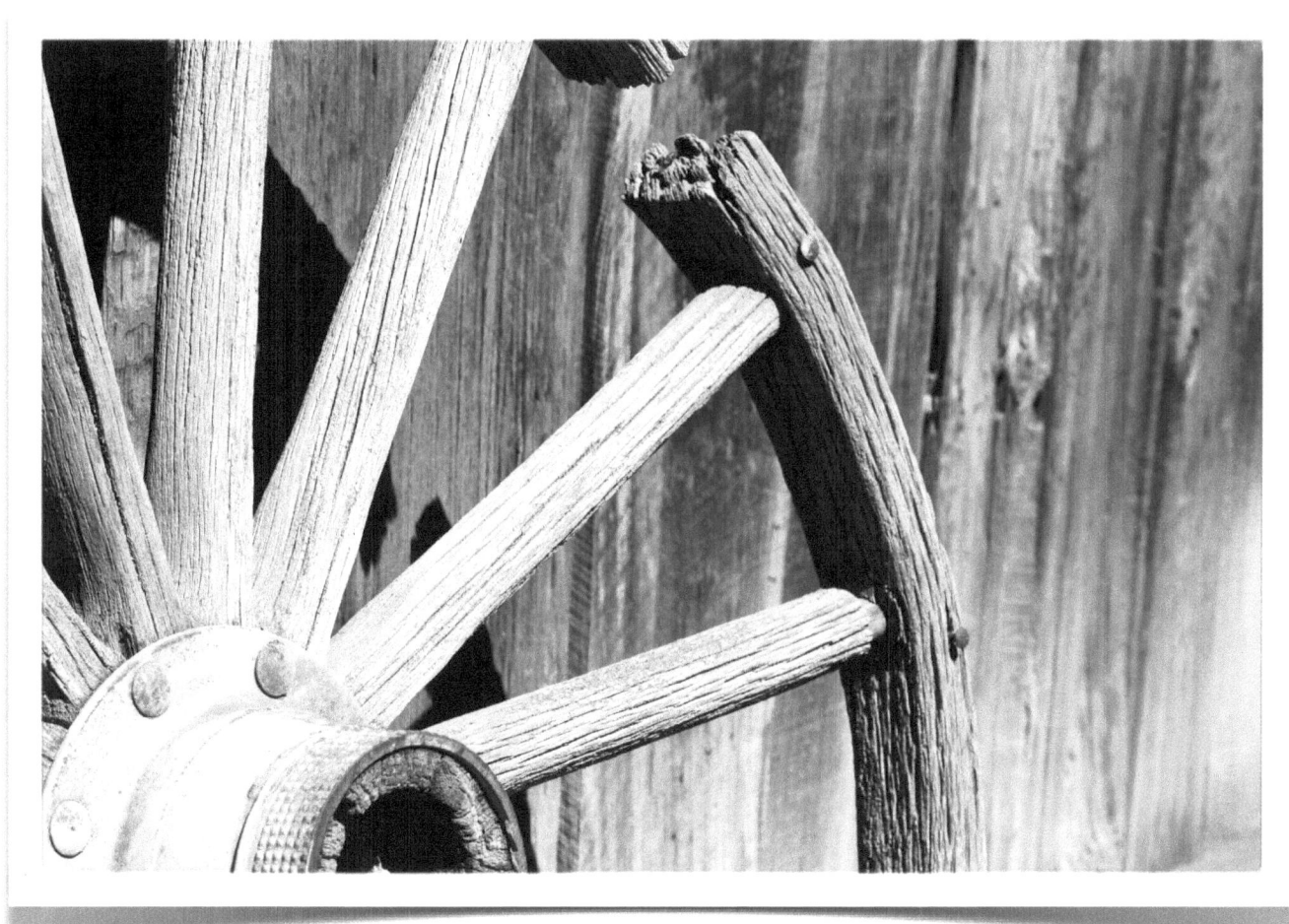

3147

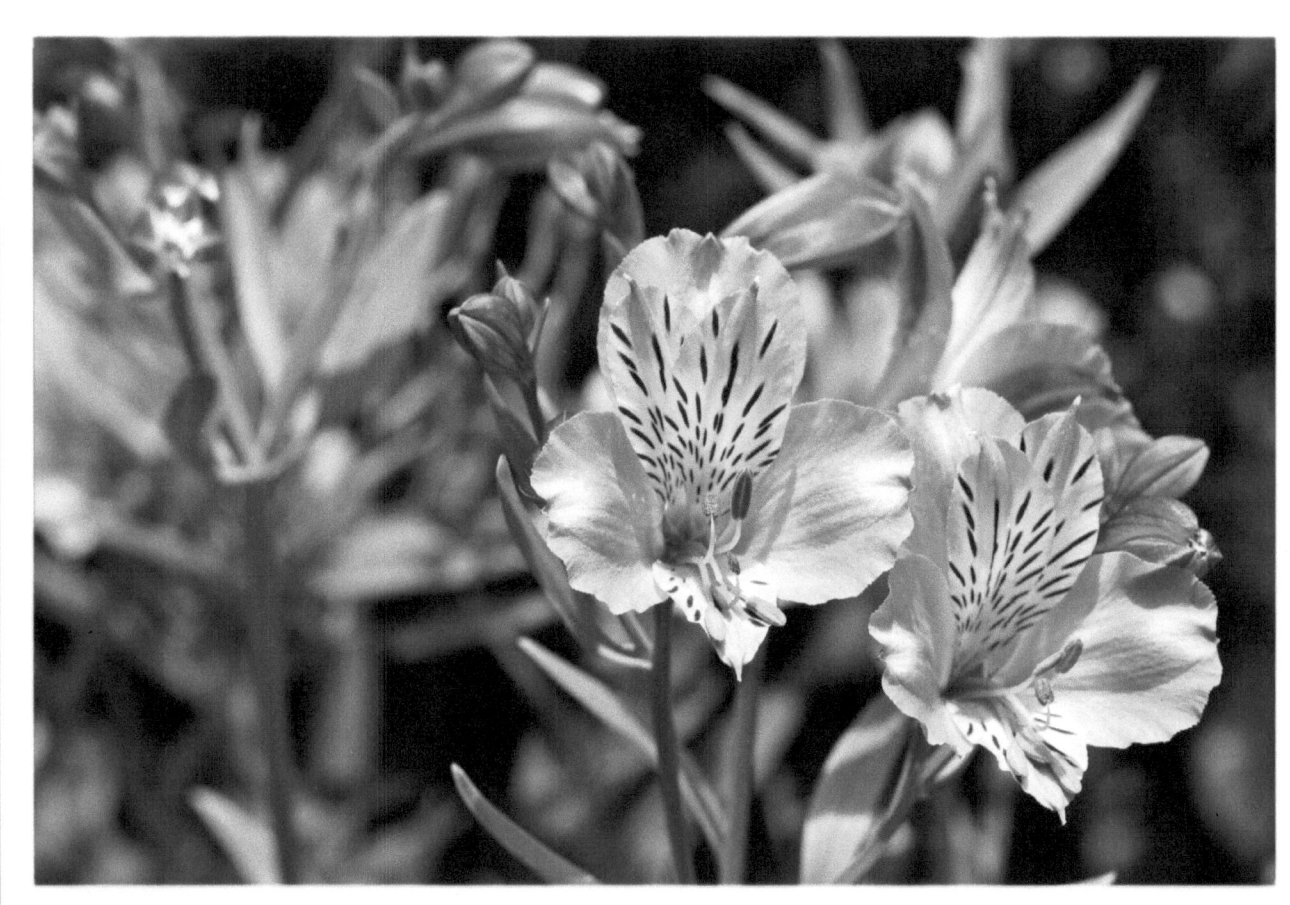

3346

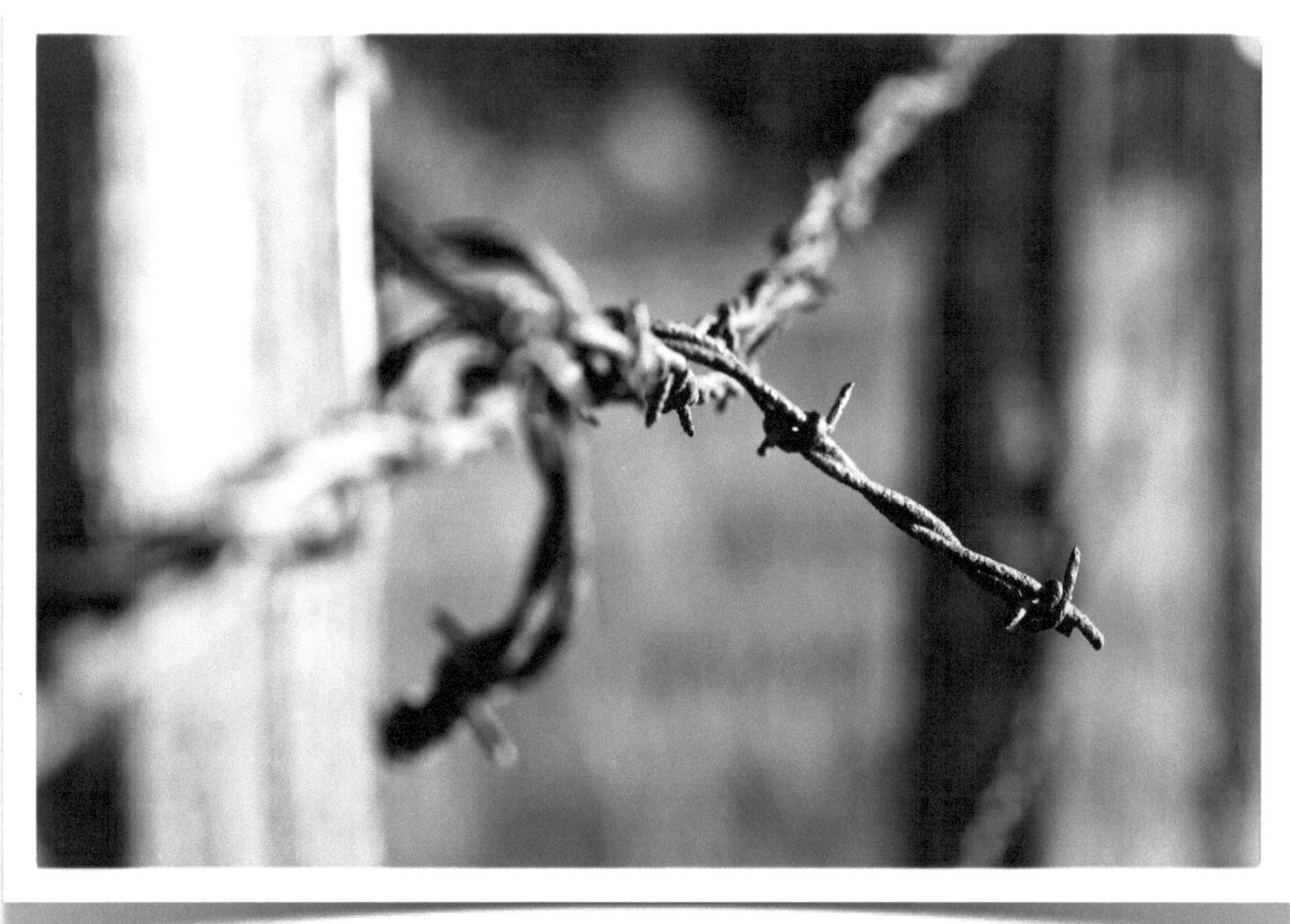

3359

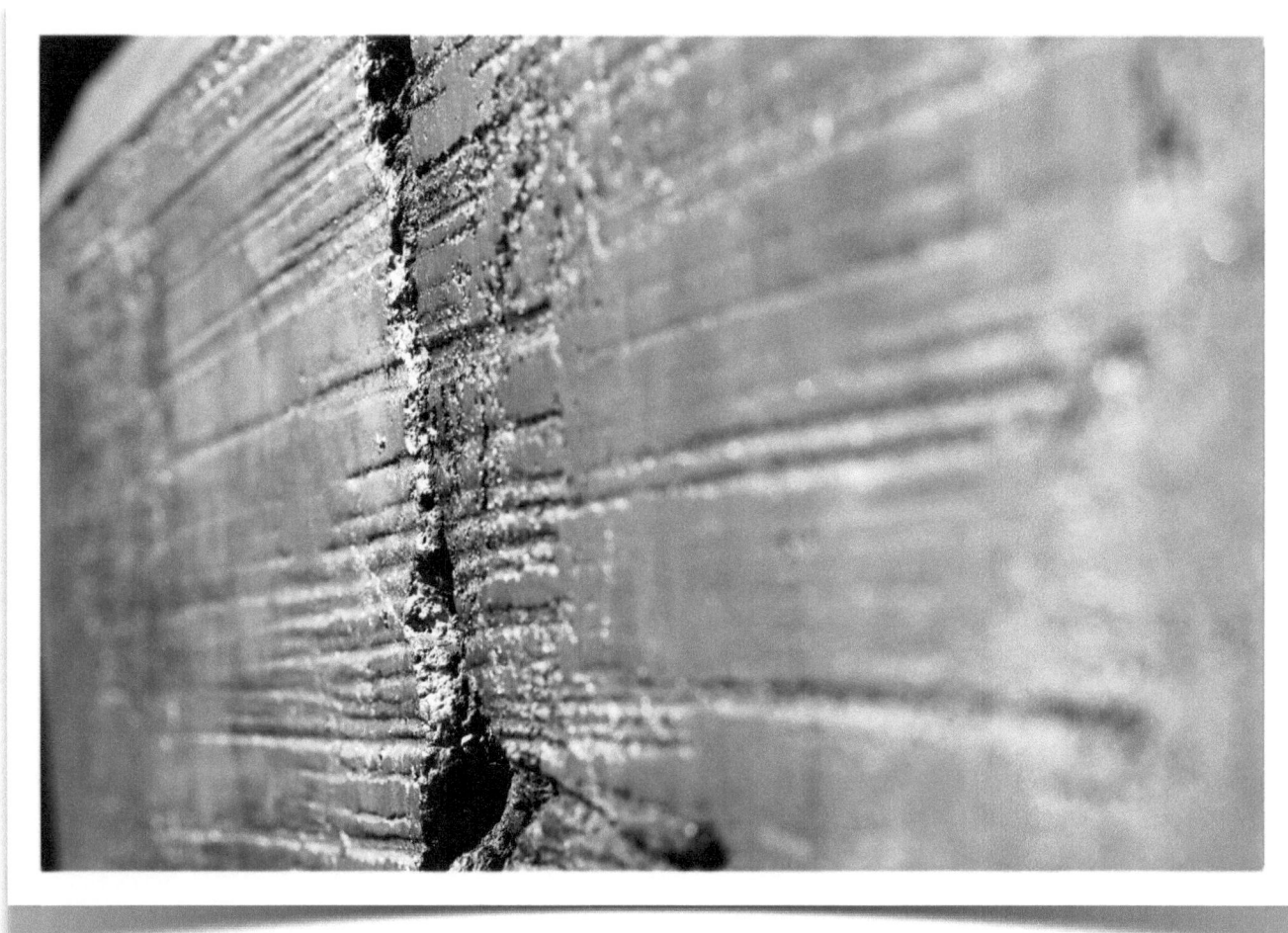

3656

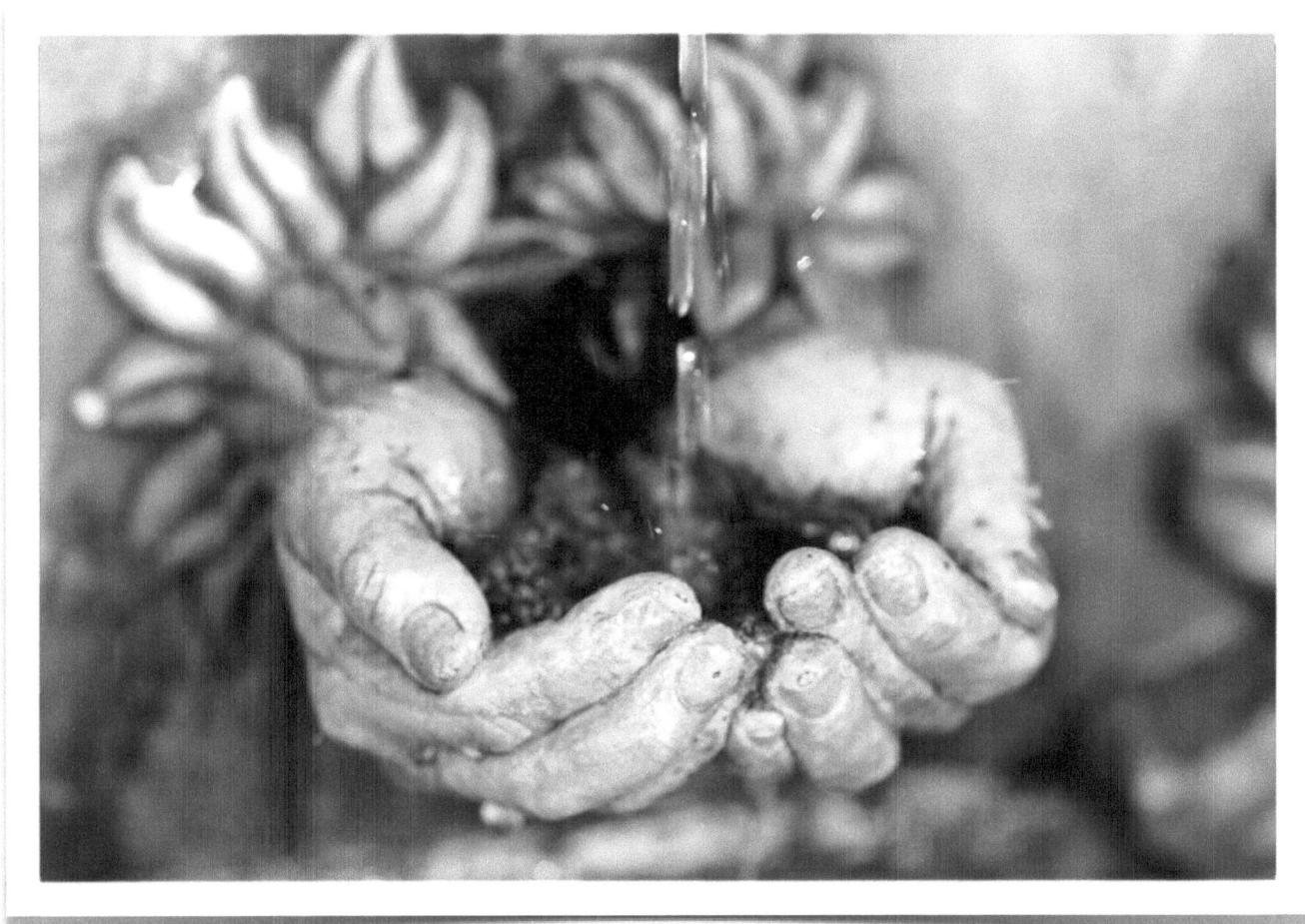

3720

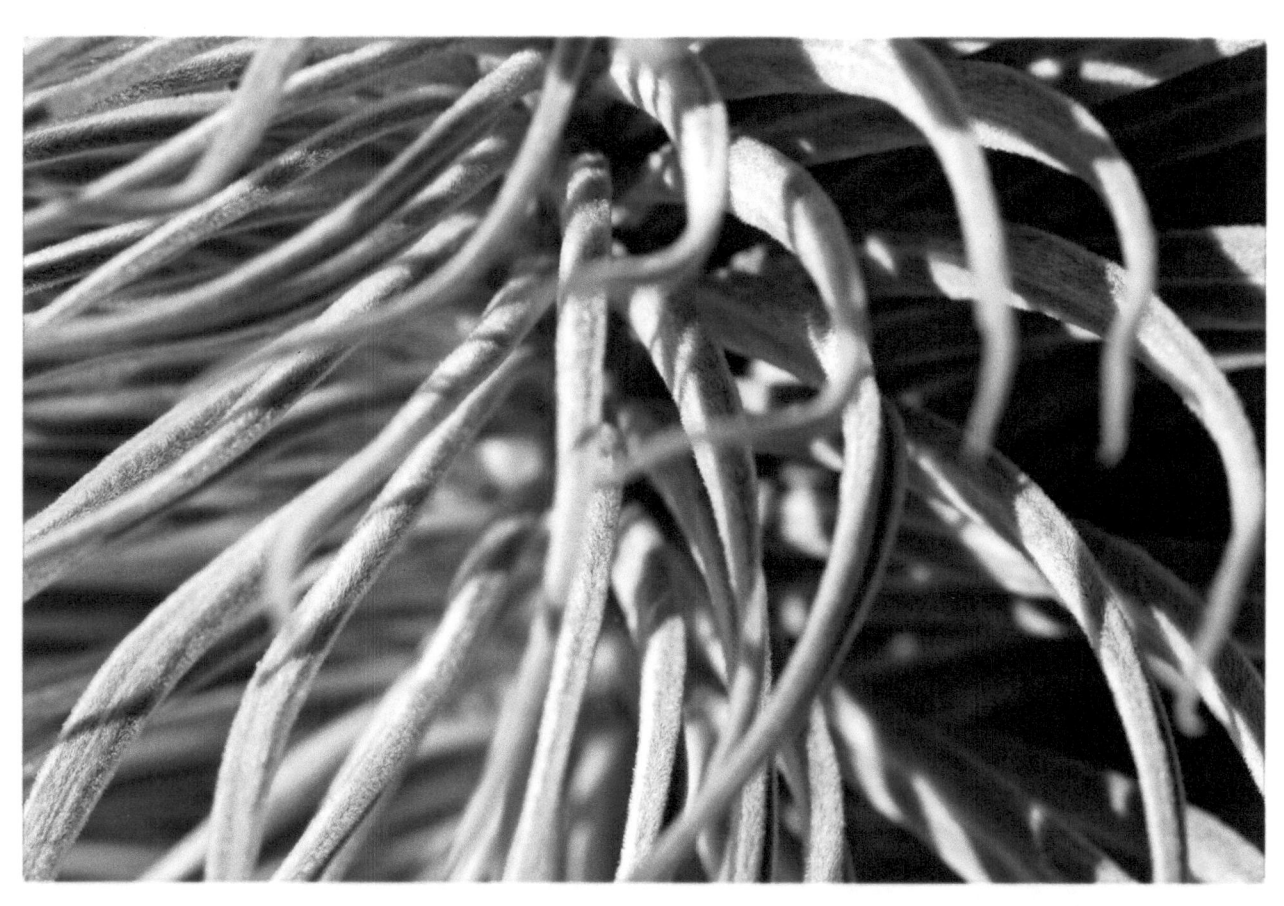

3752

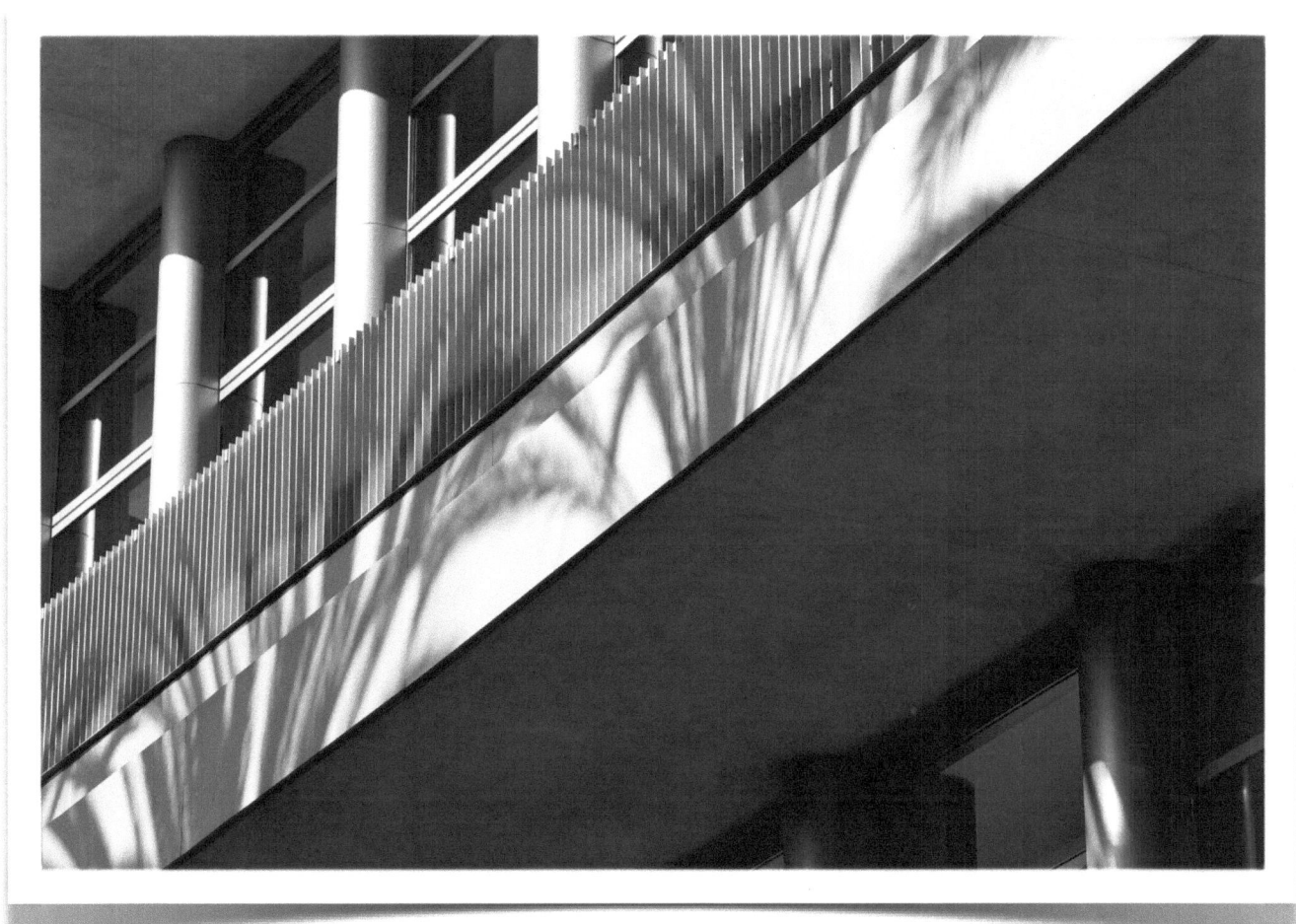

3916

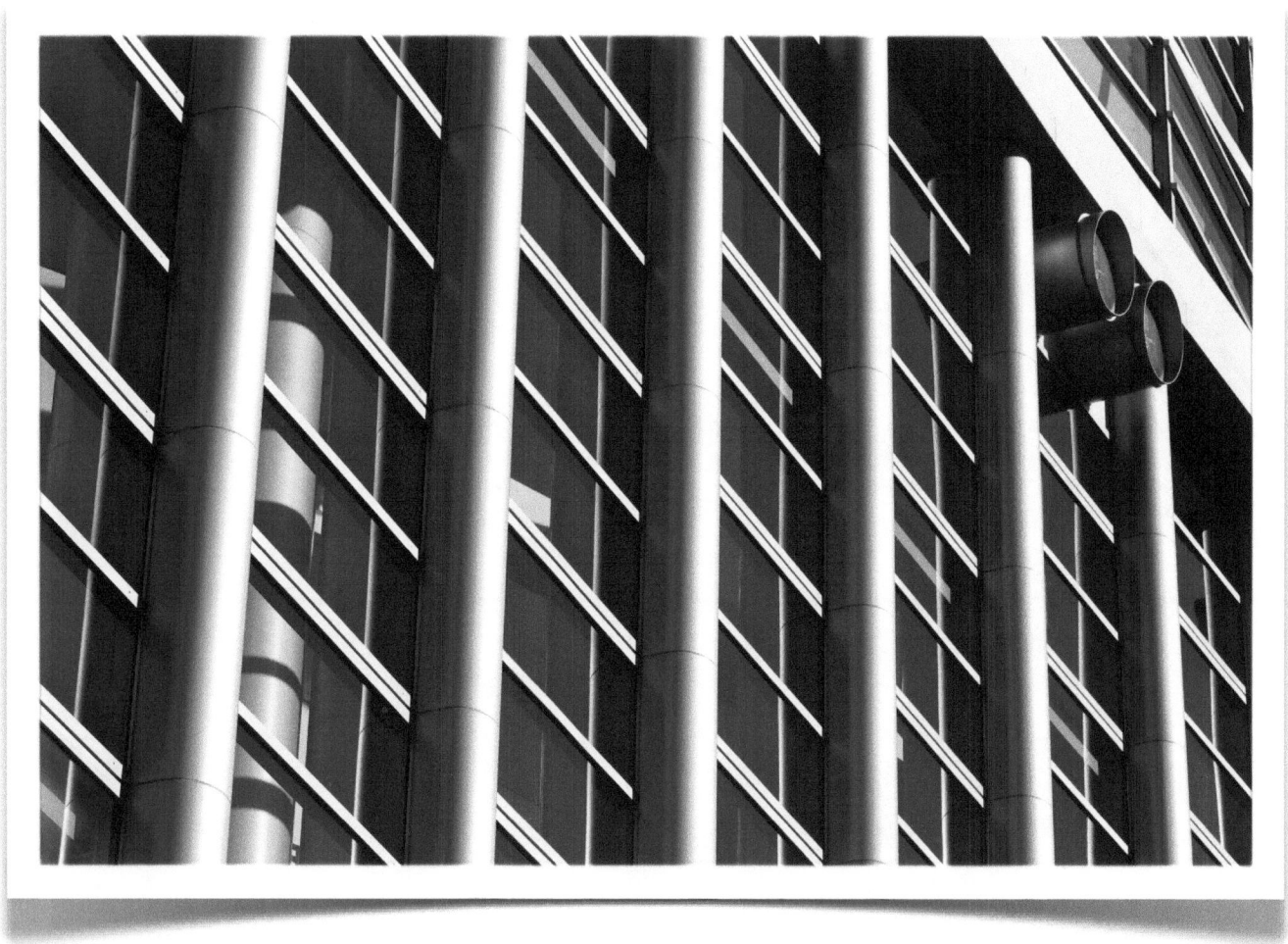

3943

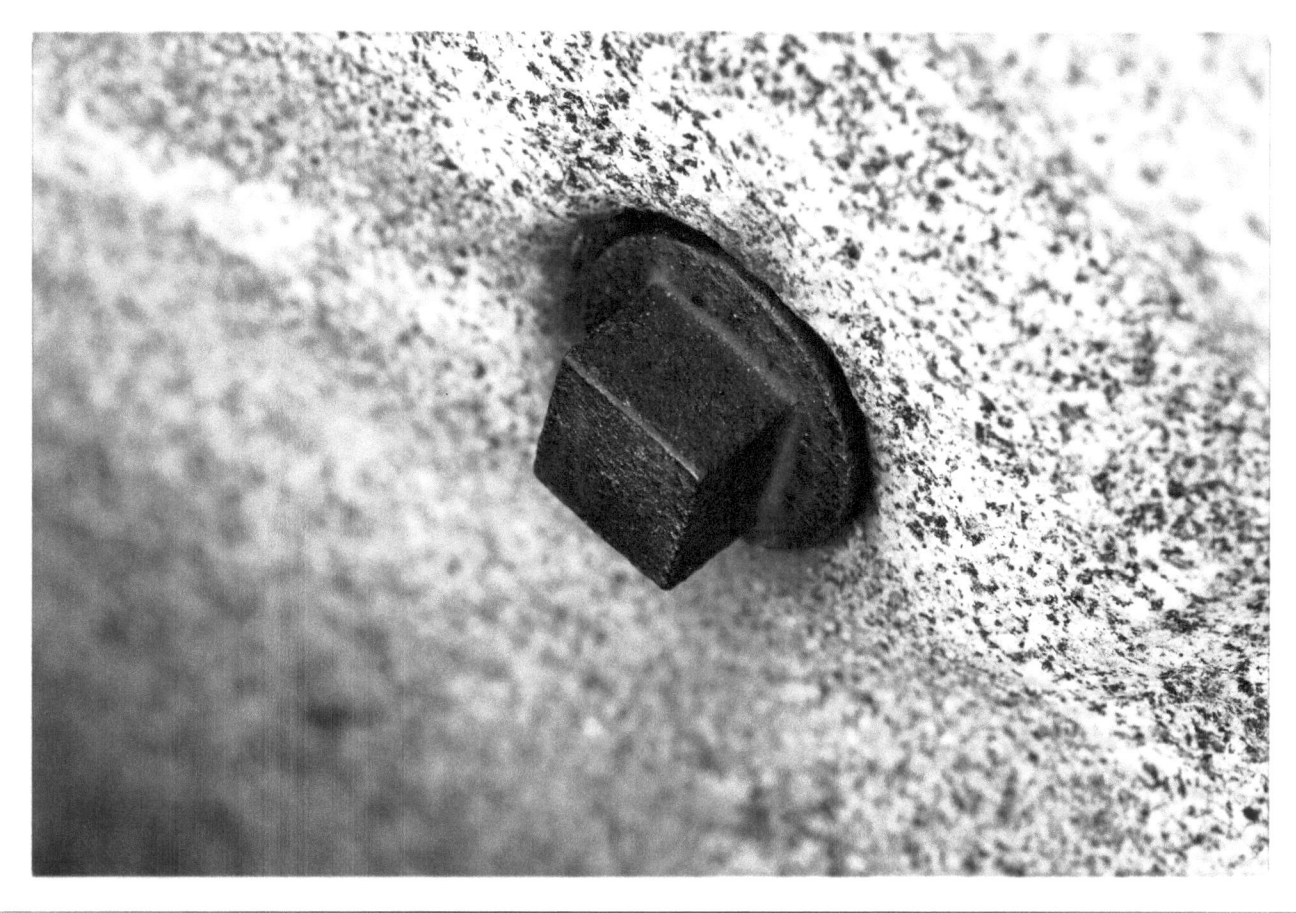

4035

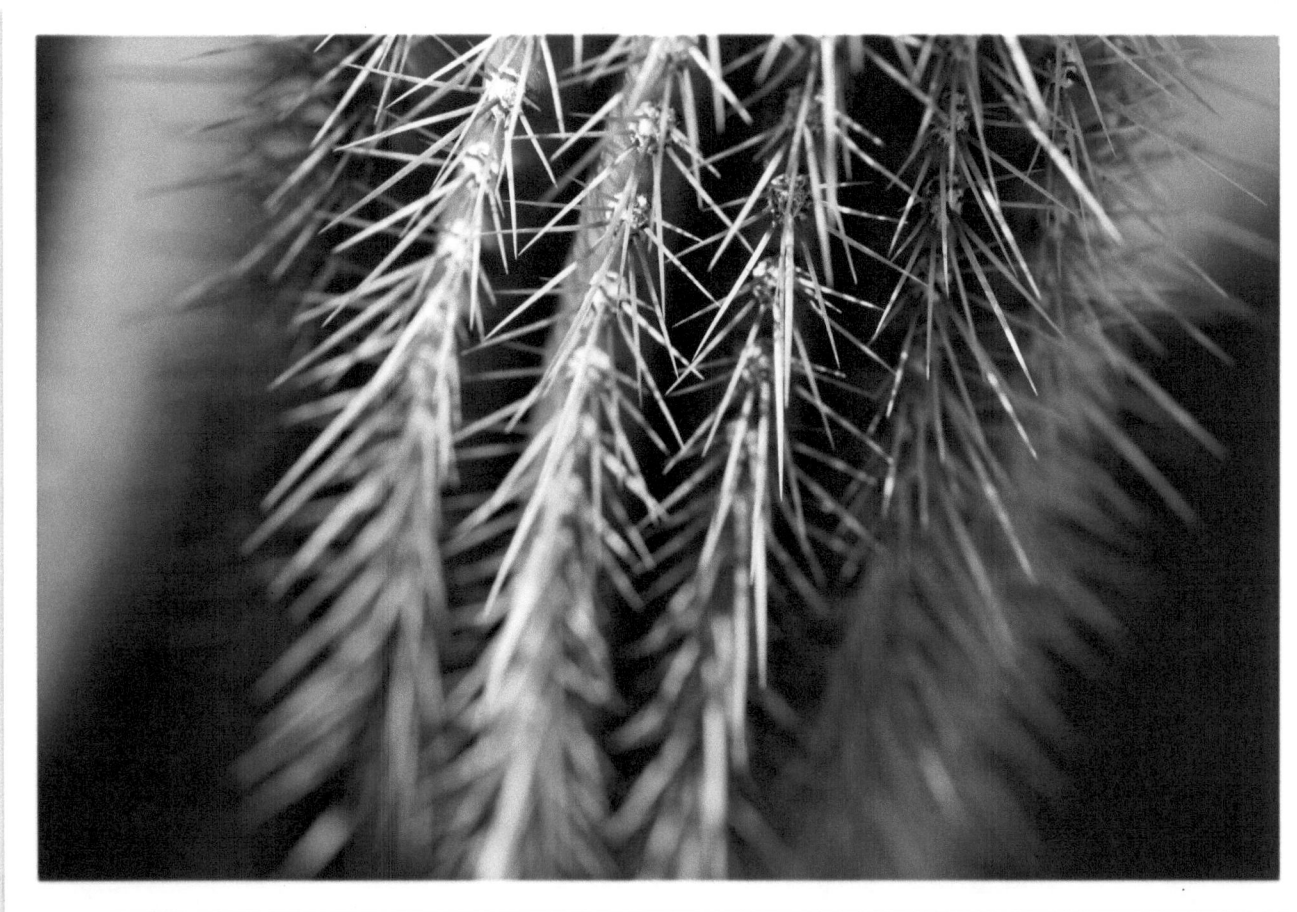

4070

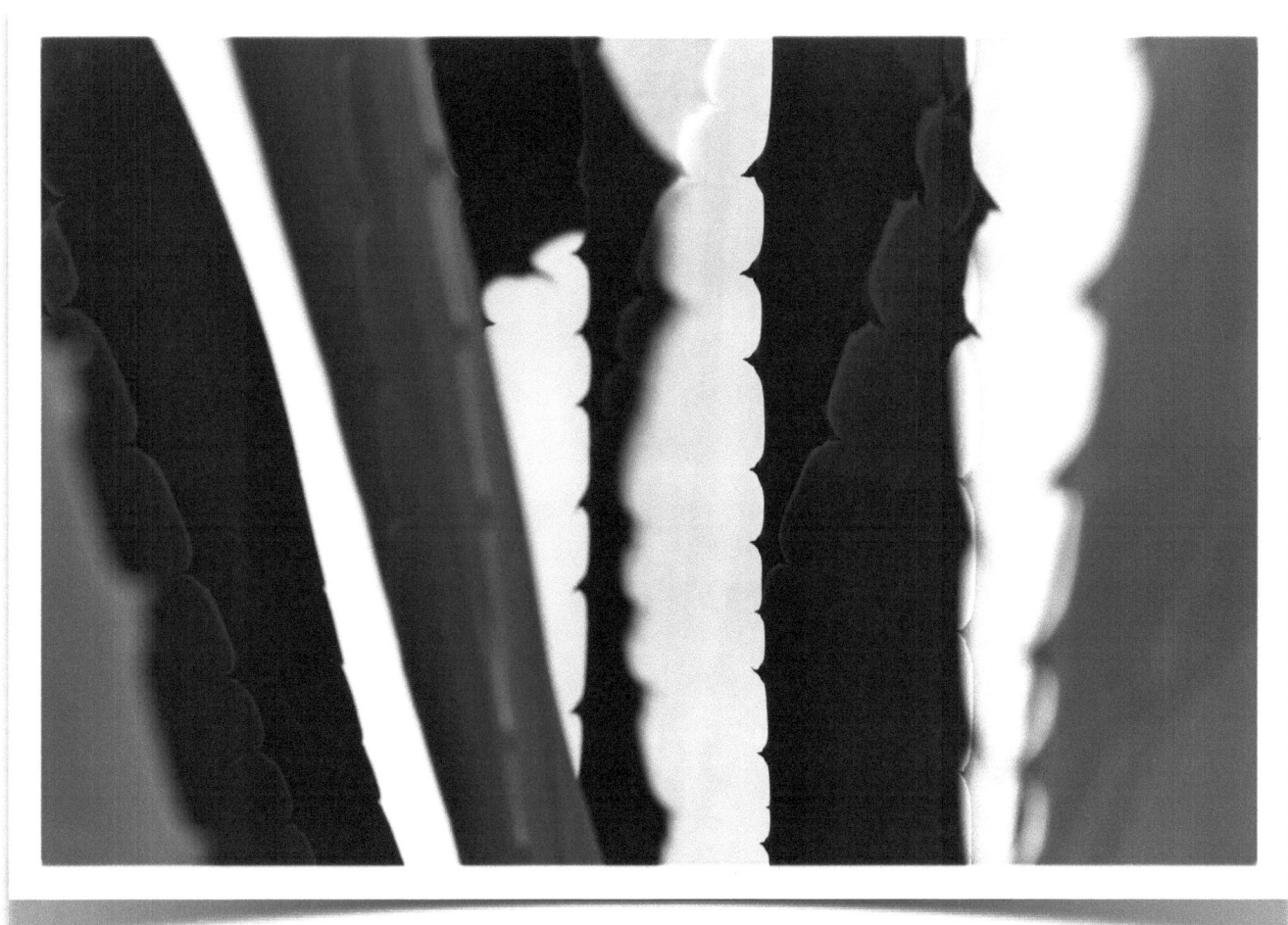

4099

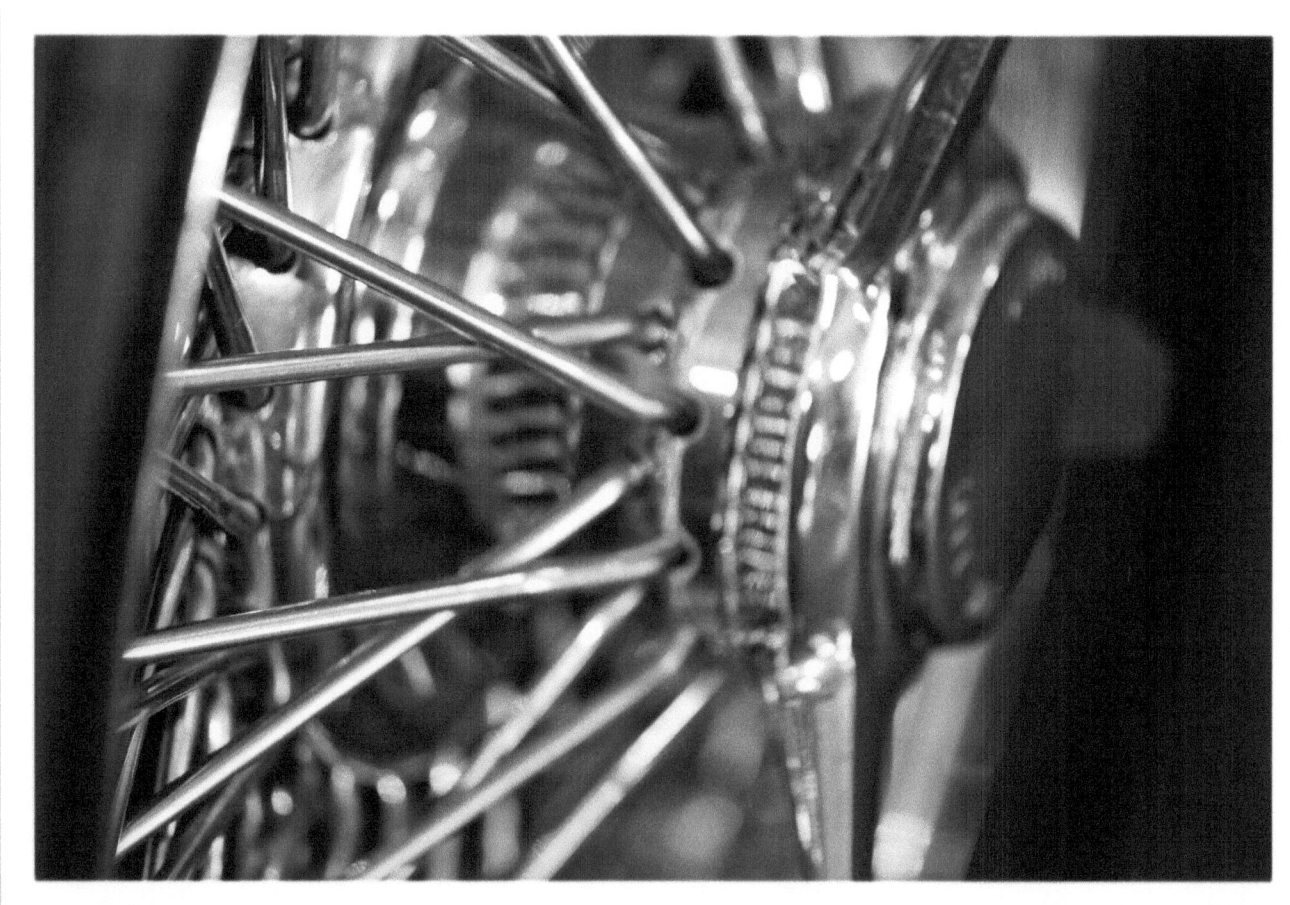

4193

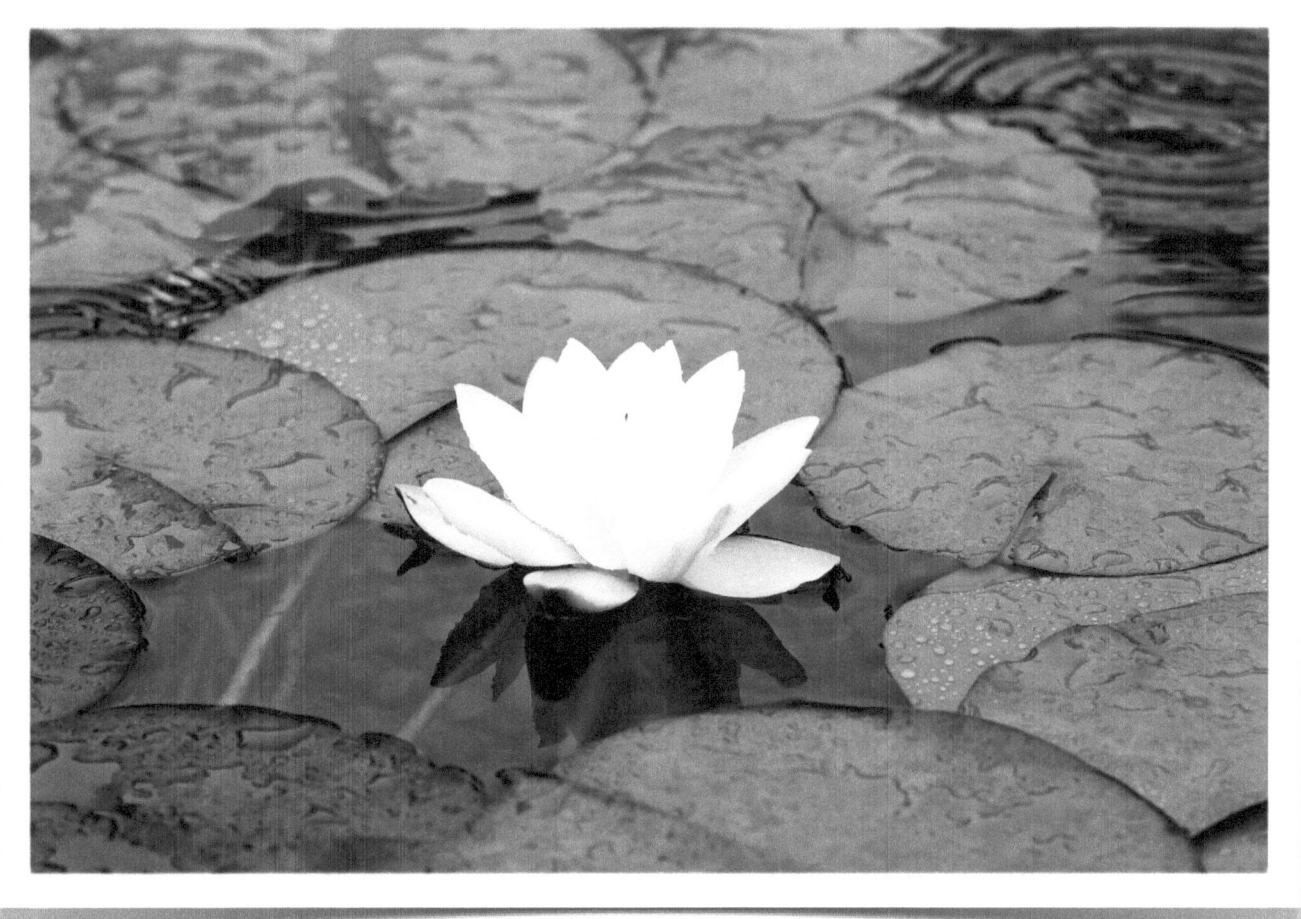

4265

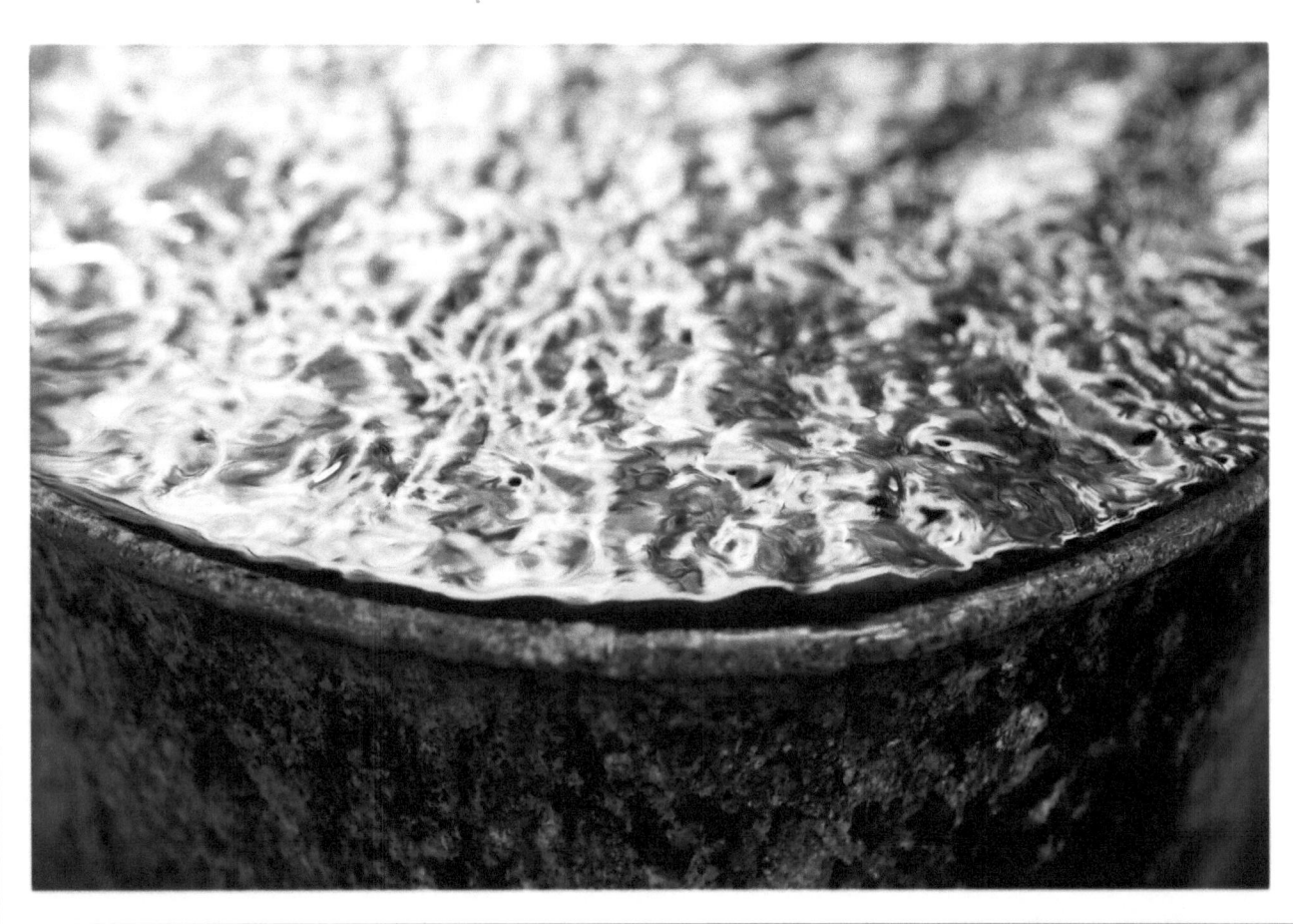

4533

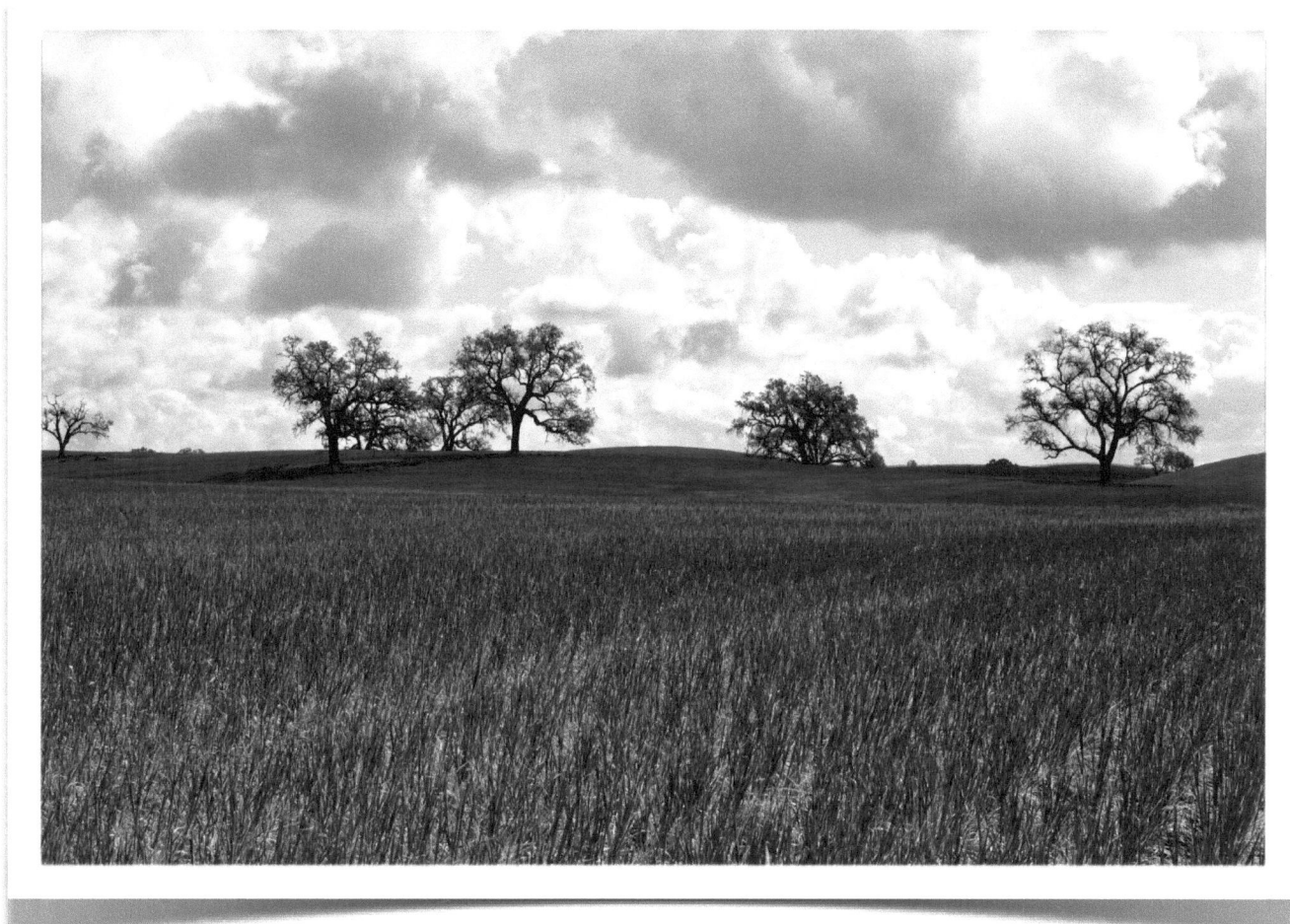

4879

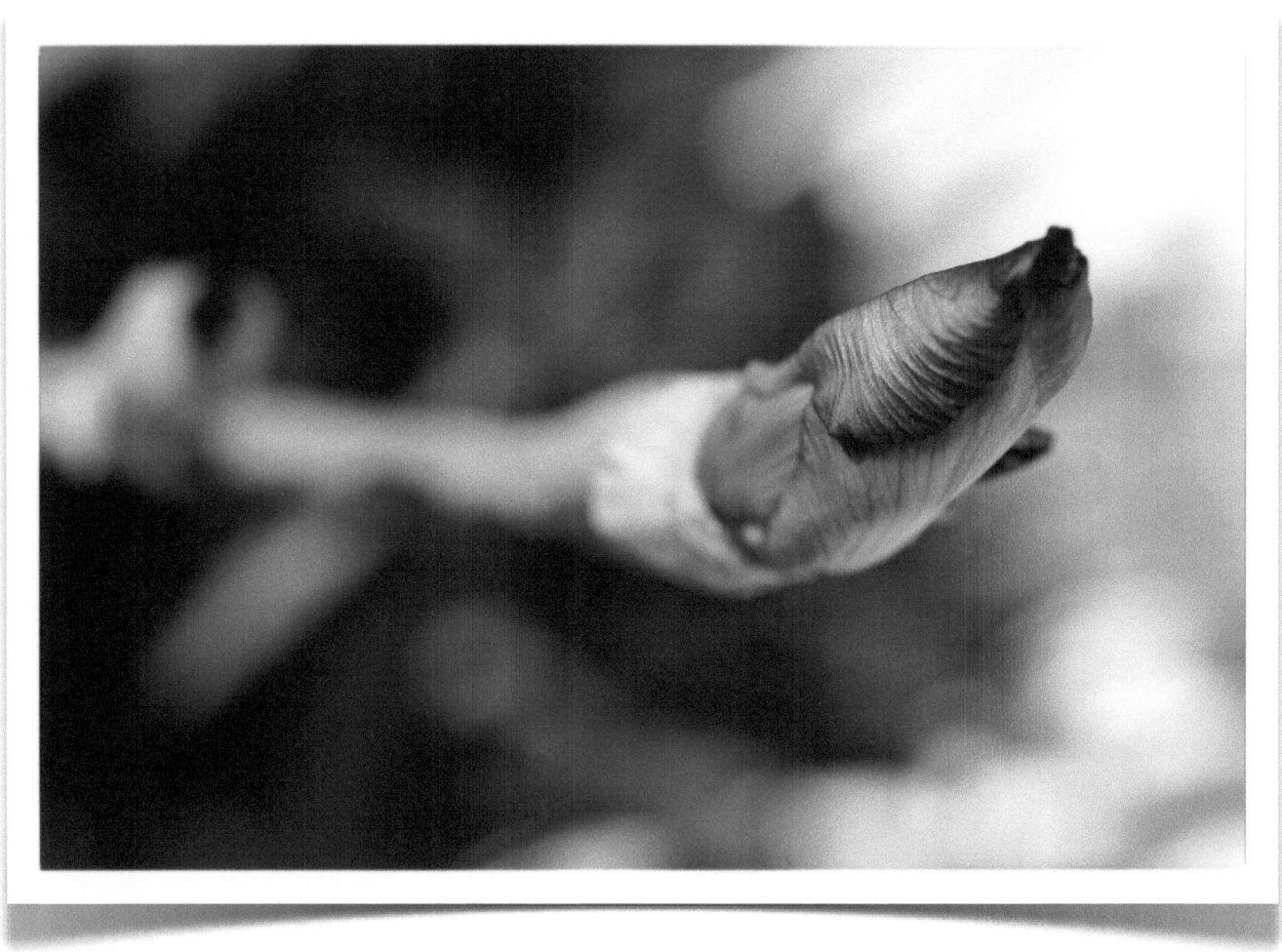

5492

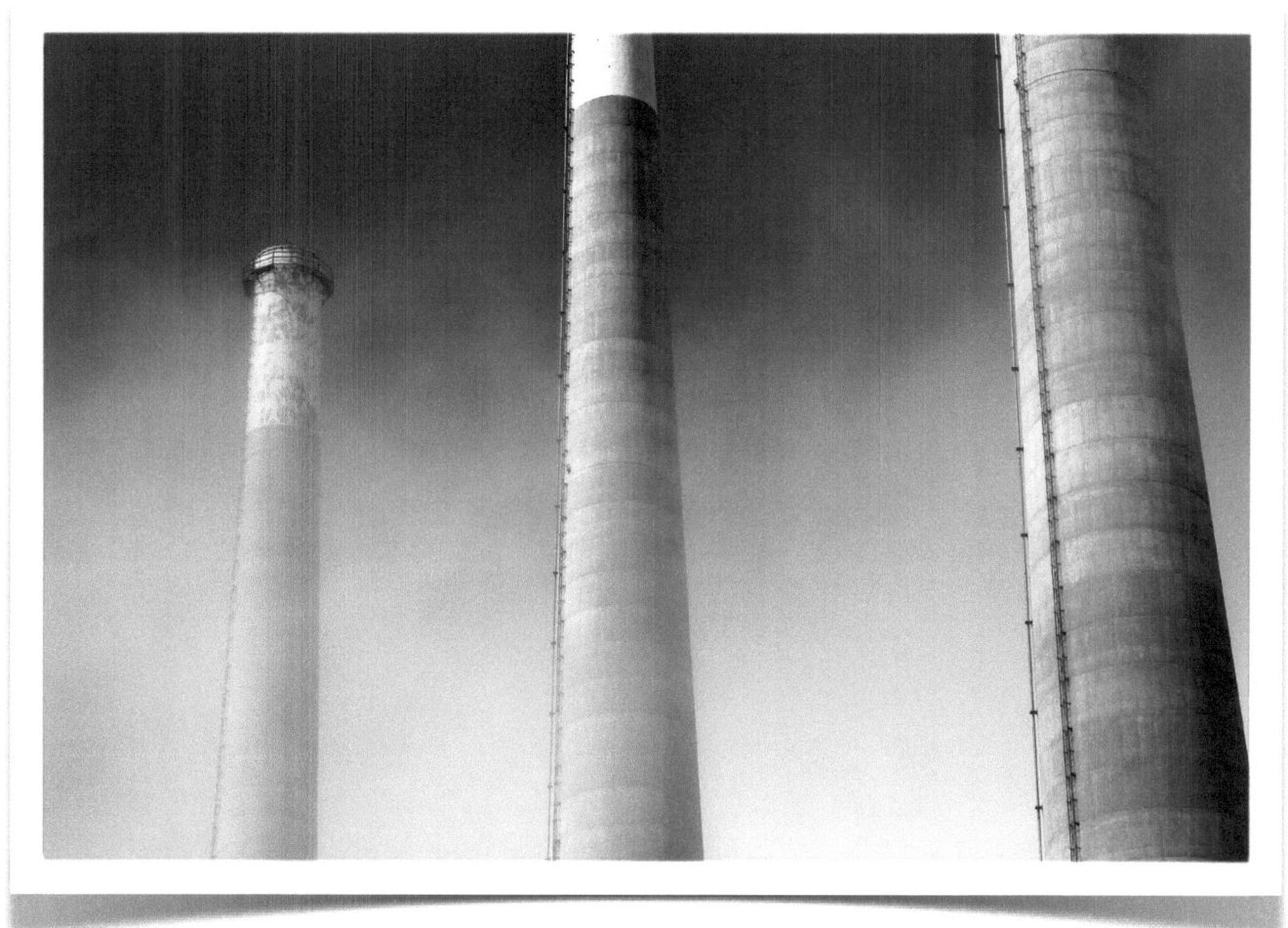

5541

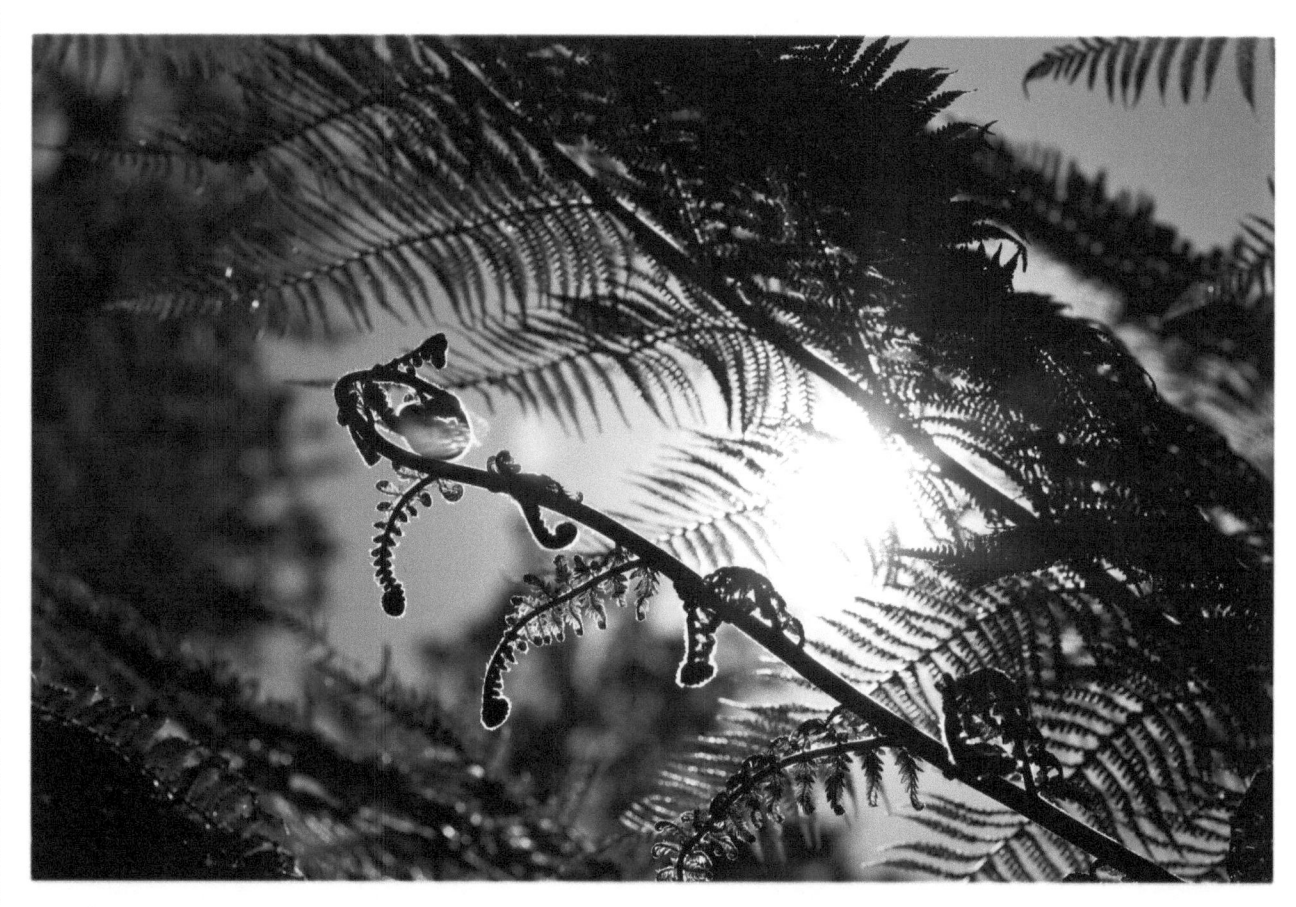

5705

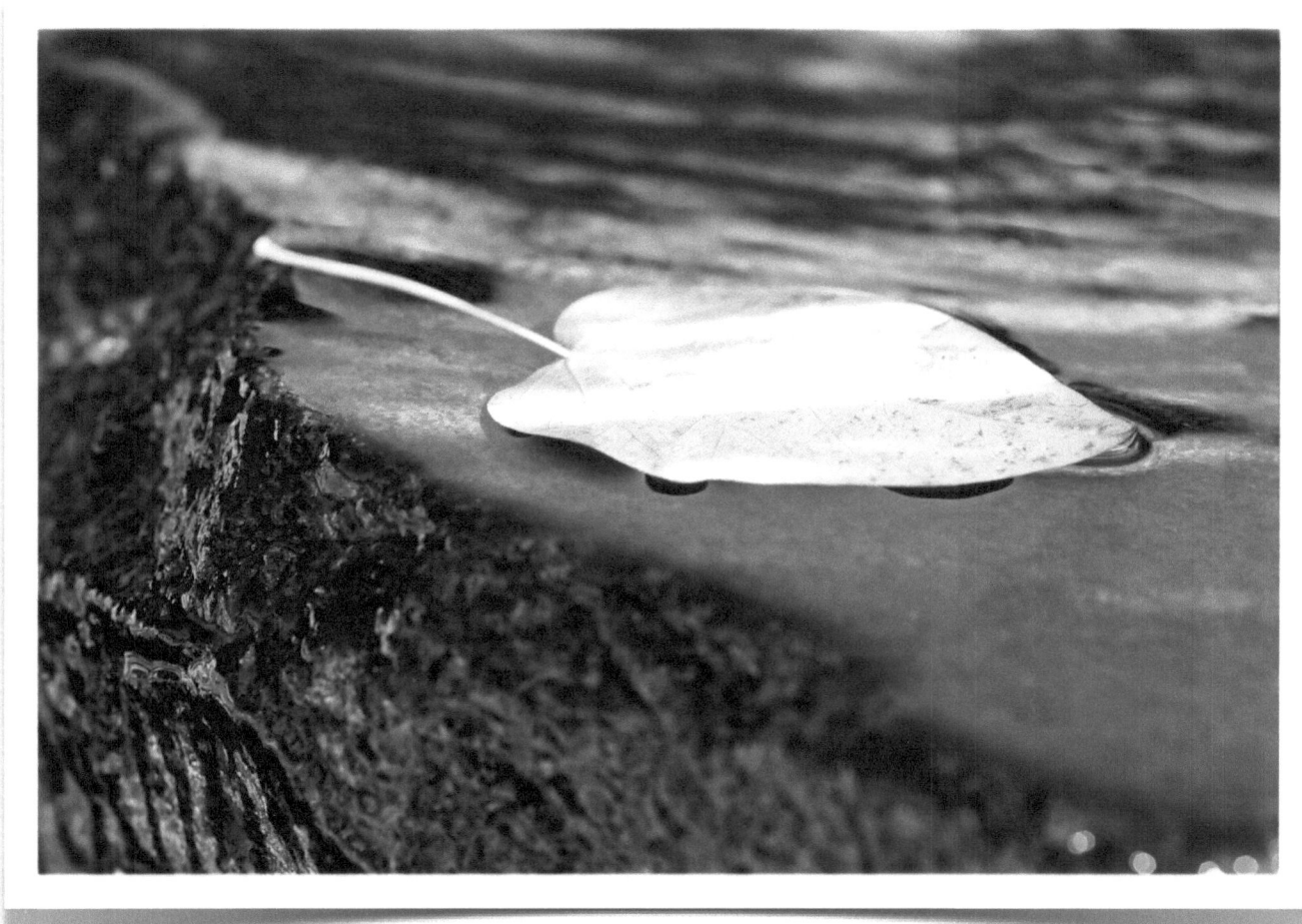

5750

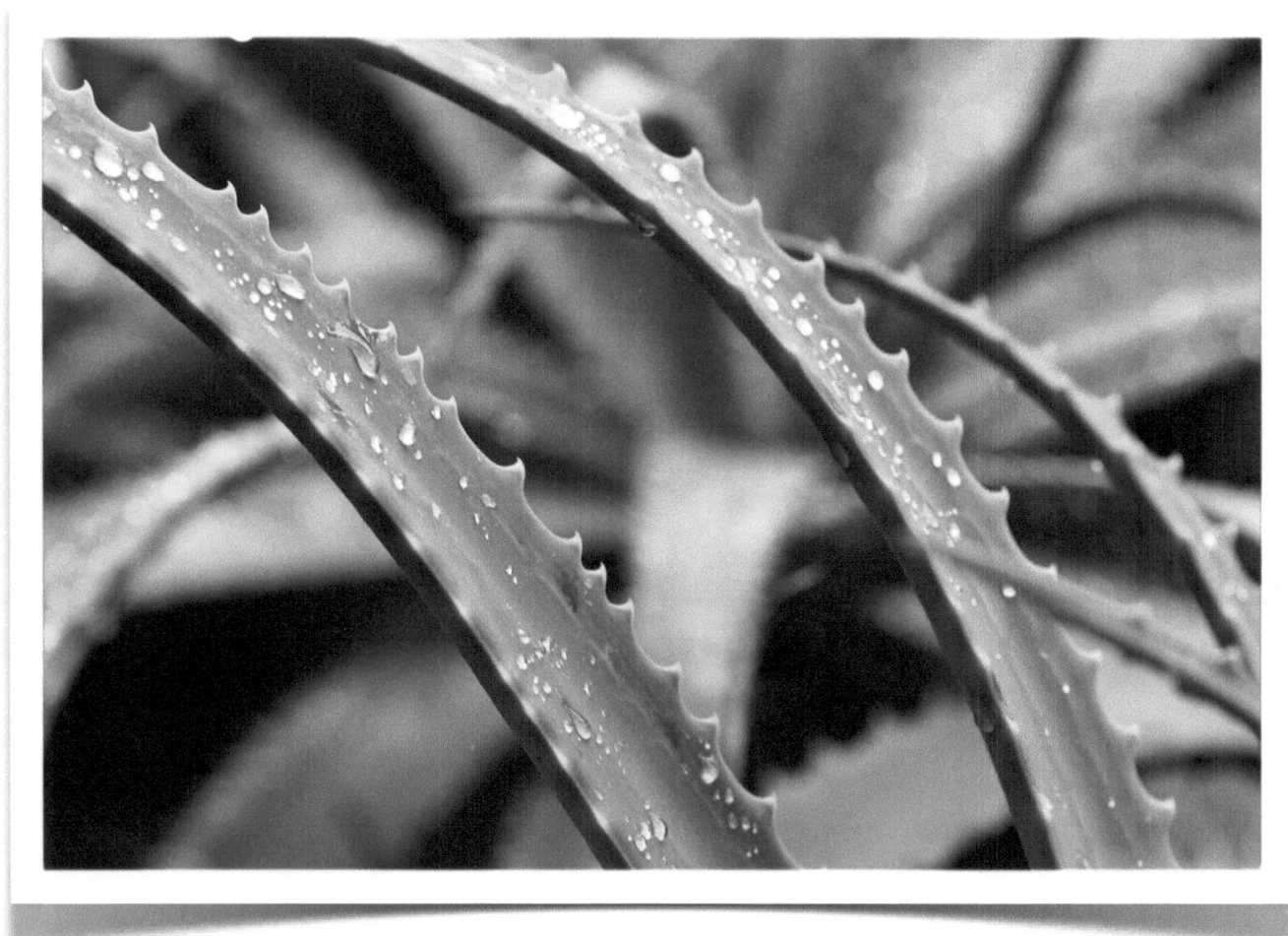

5784

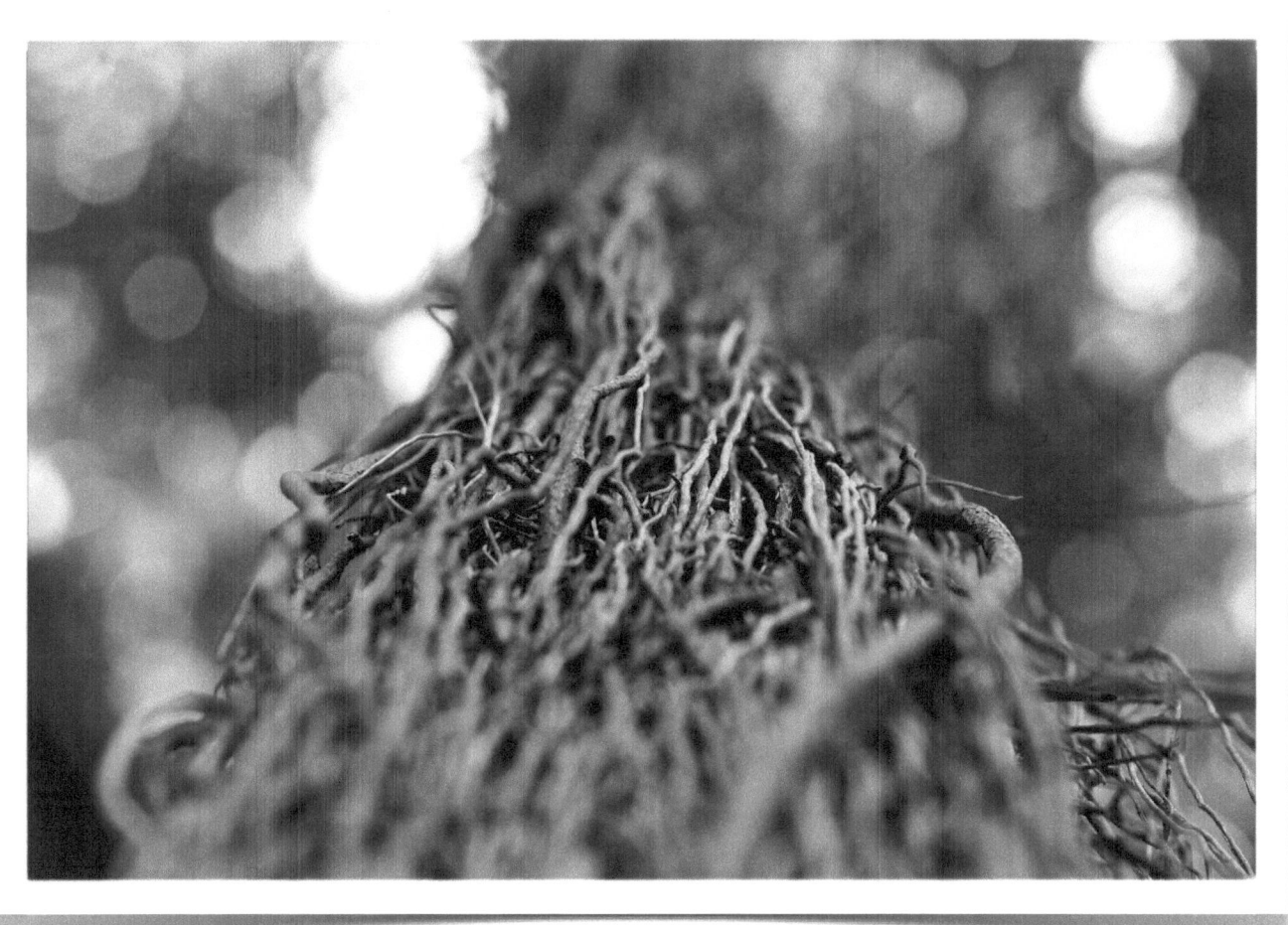

5811

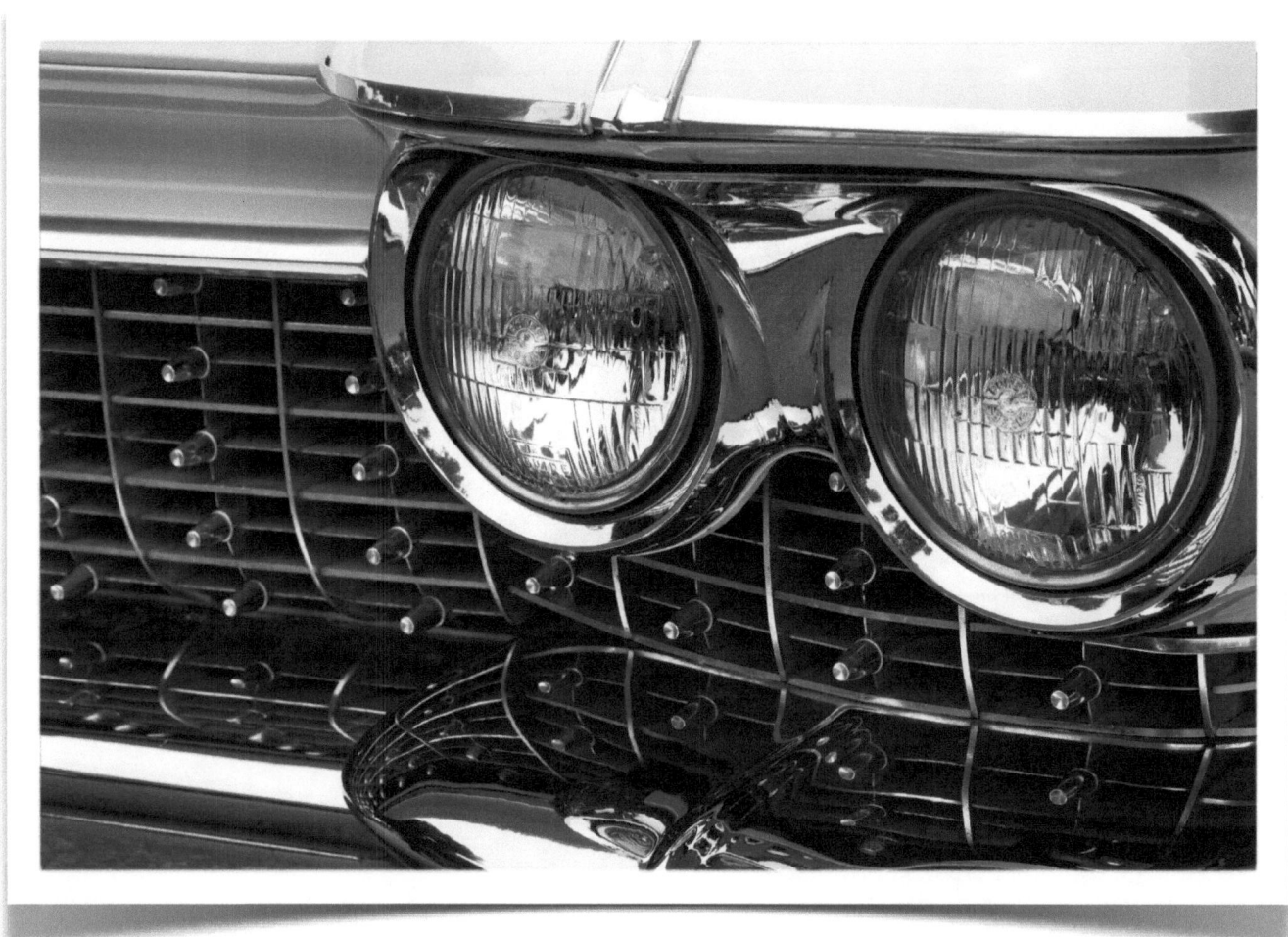

5844

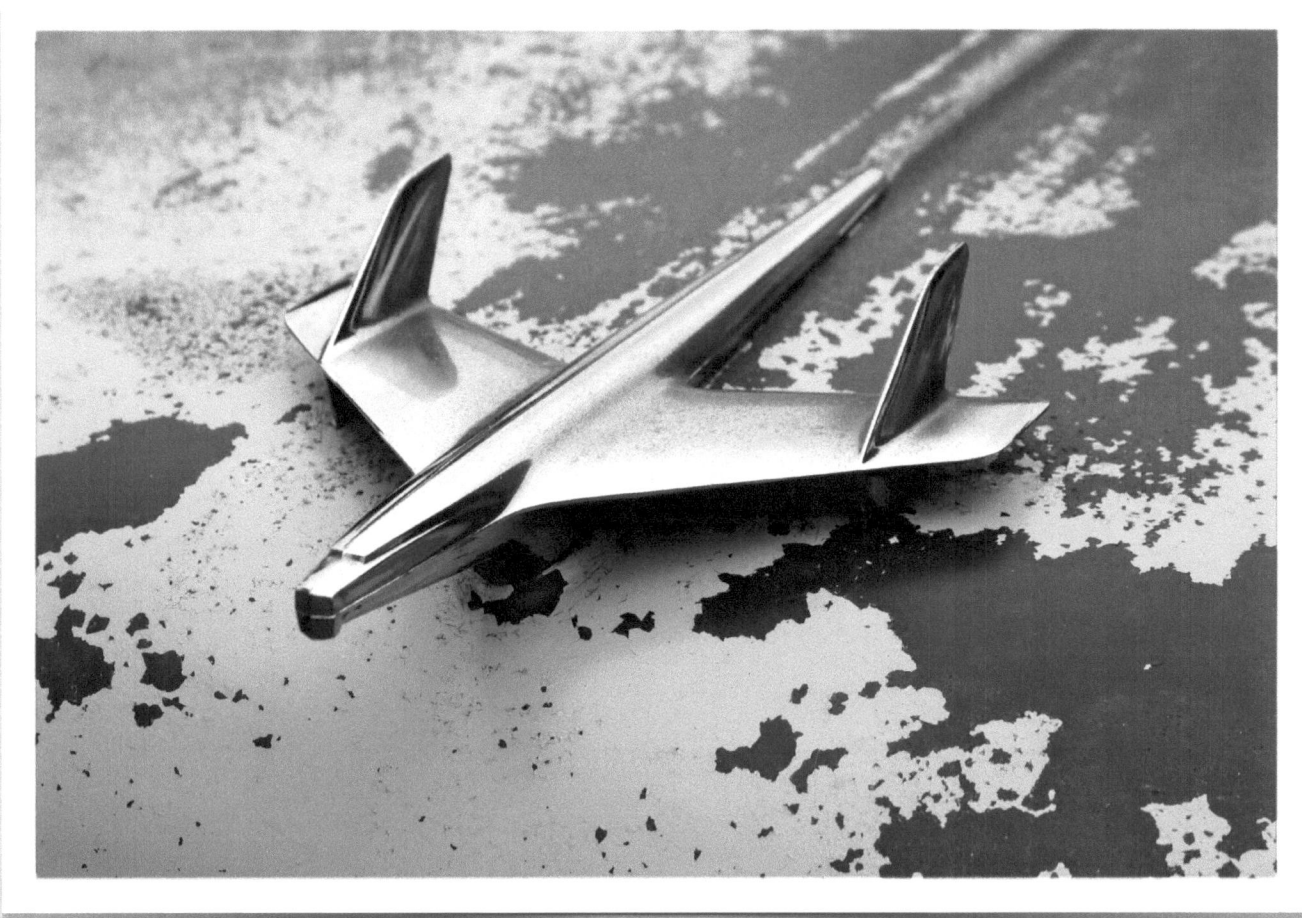

5846

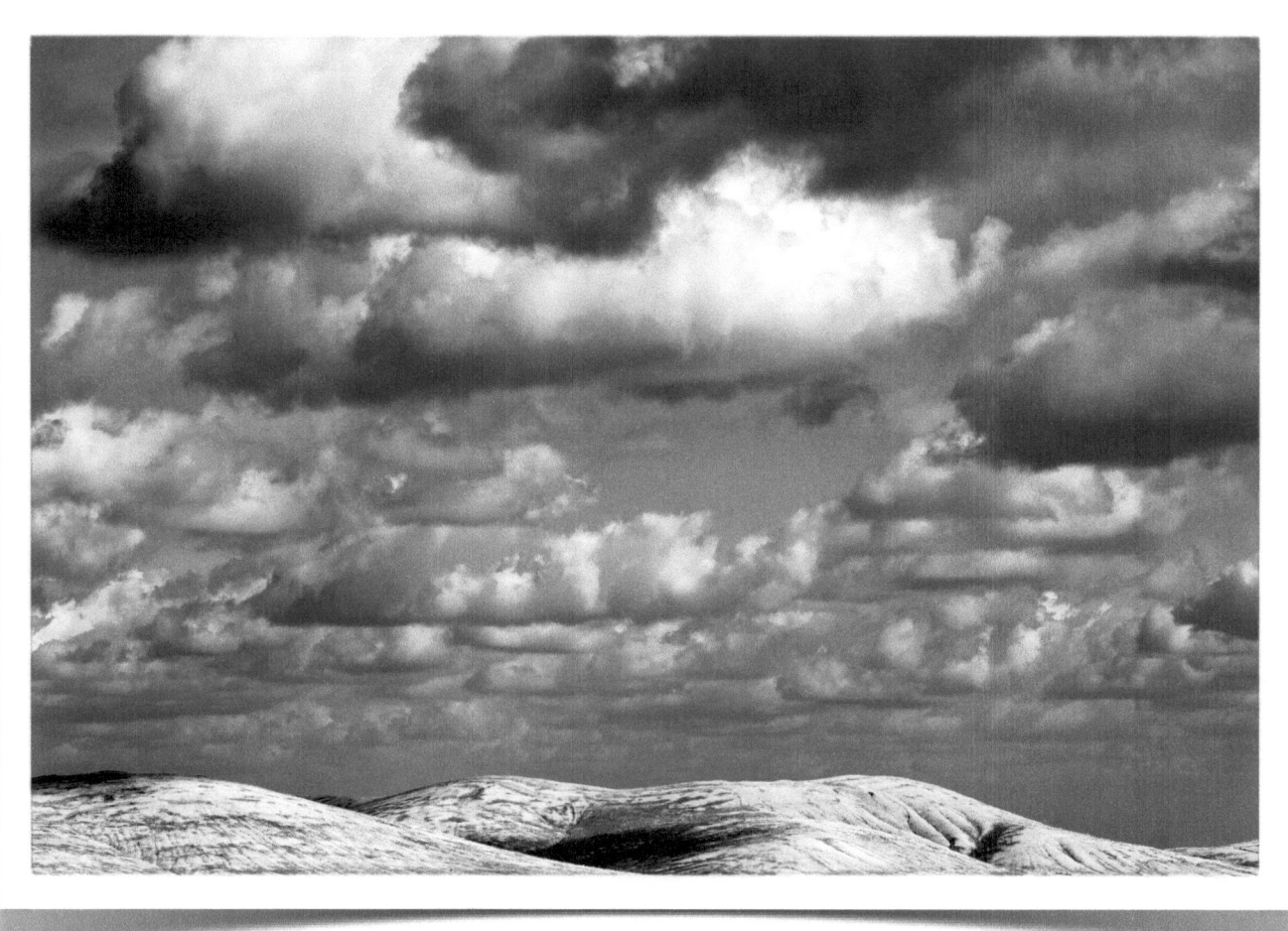

5992

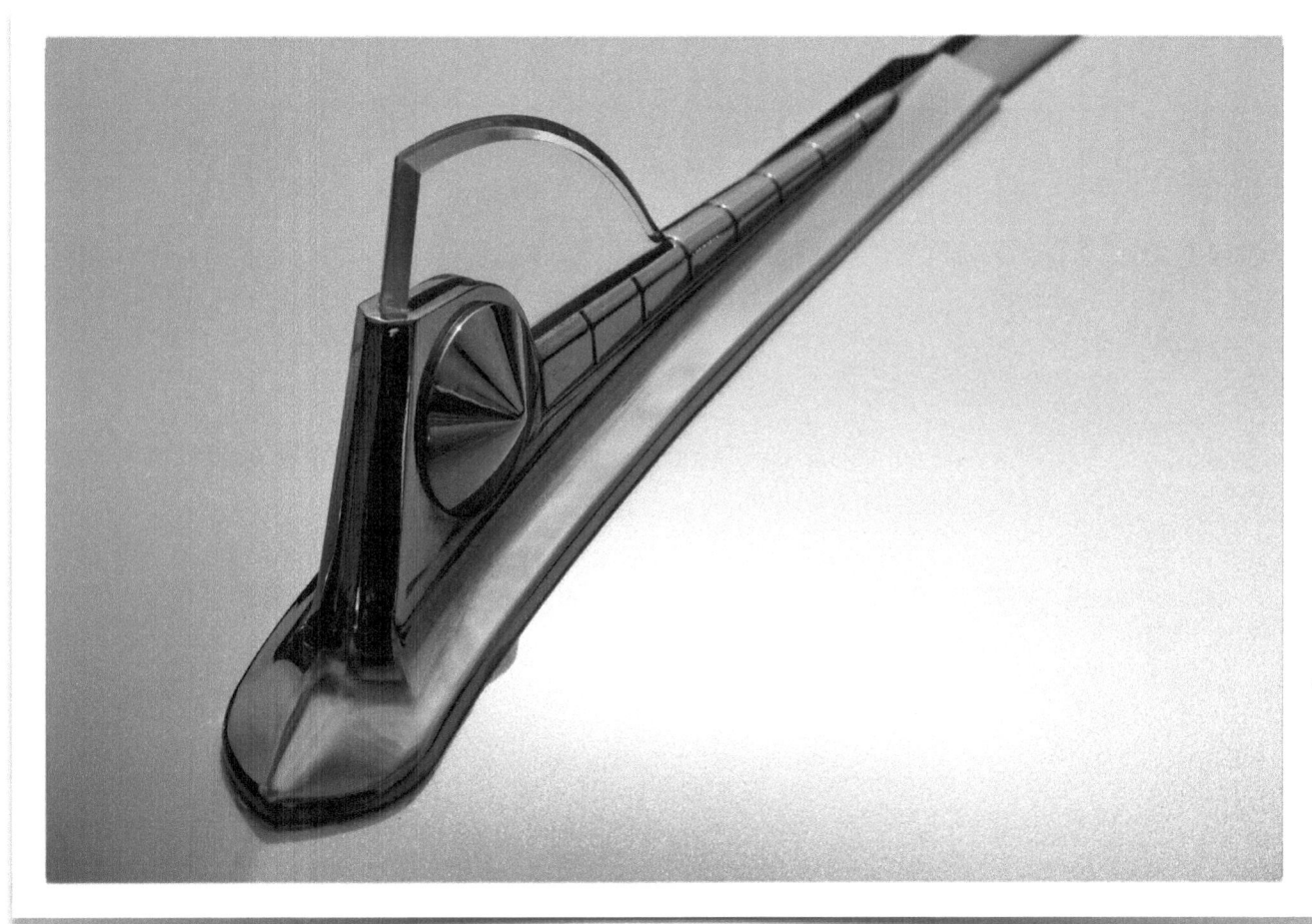

6014

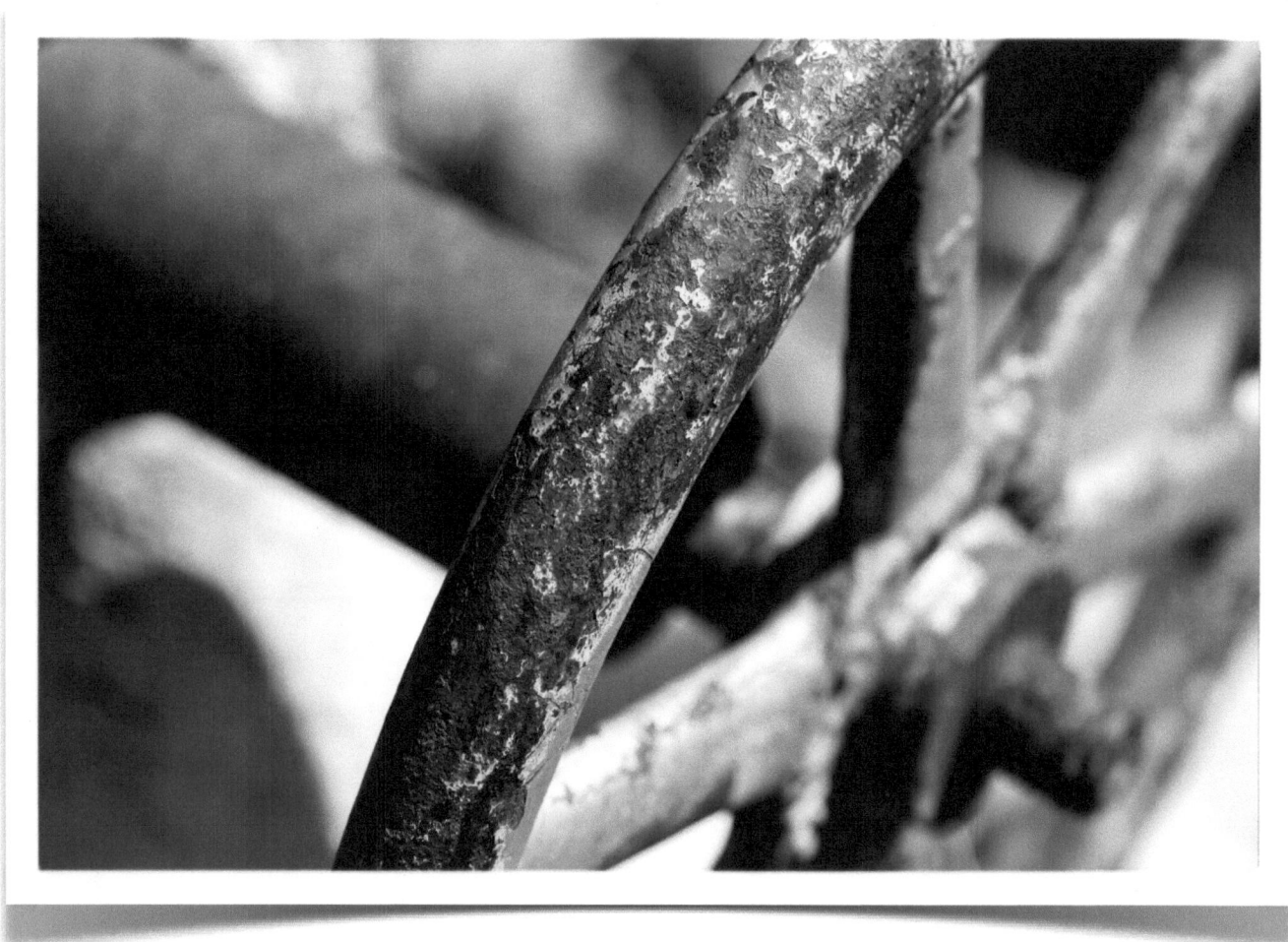

6095

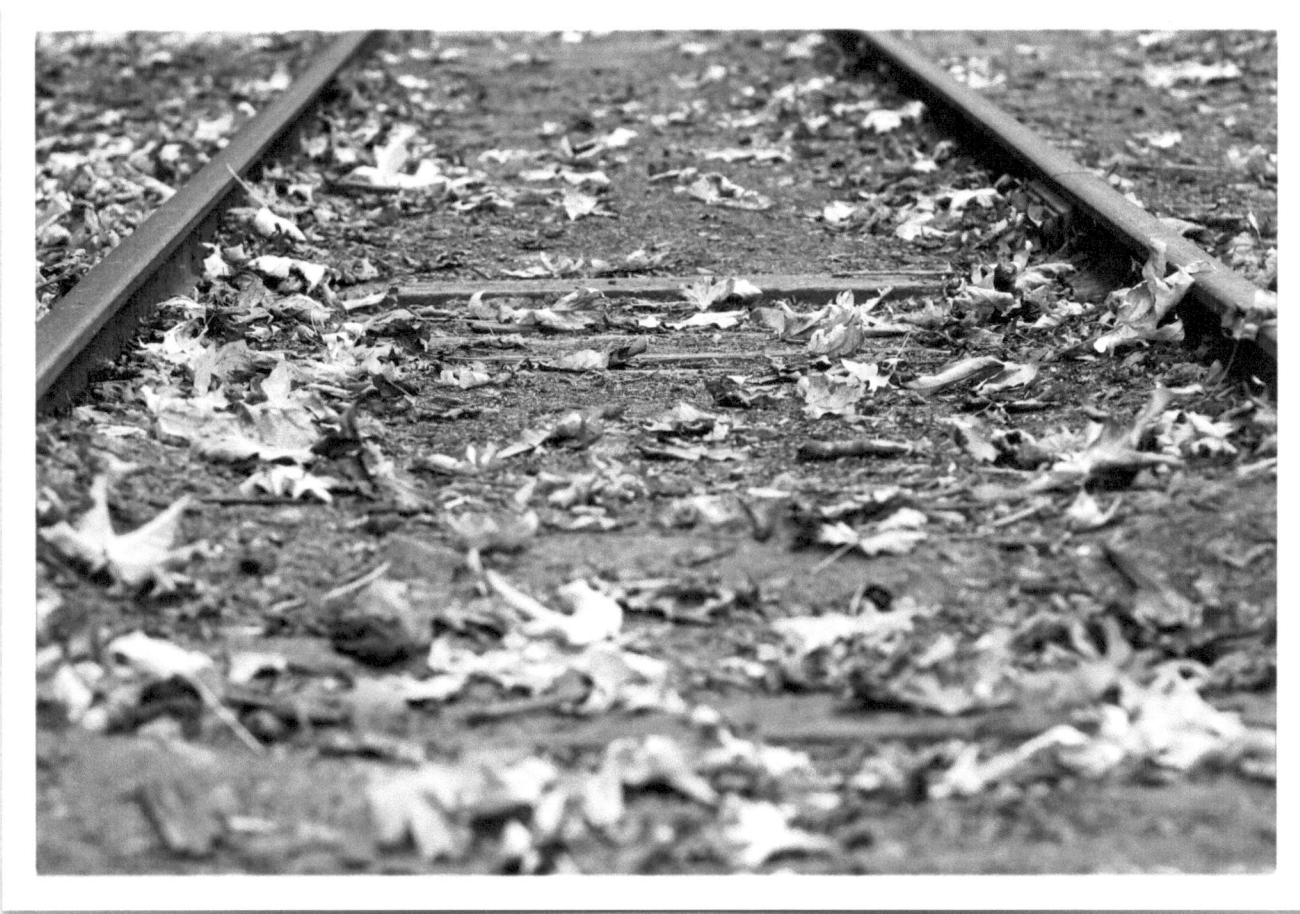

6176

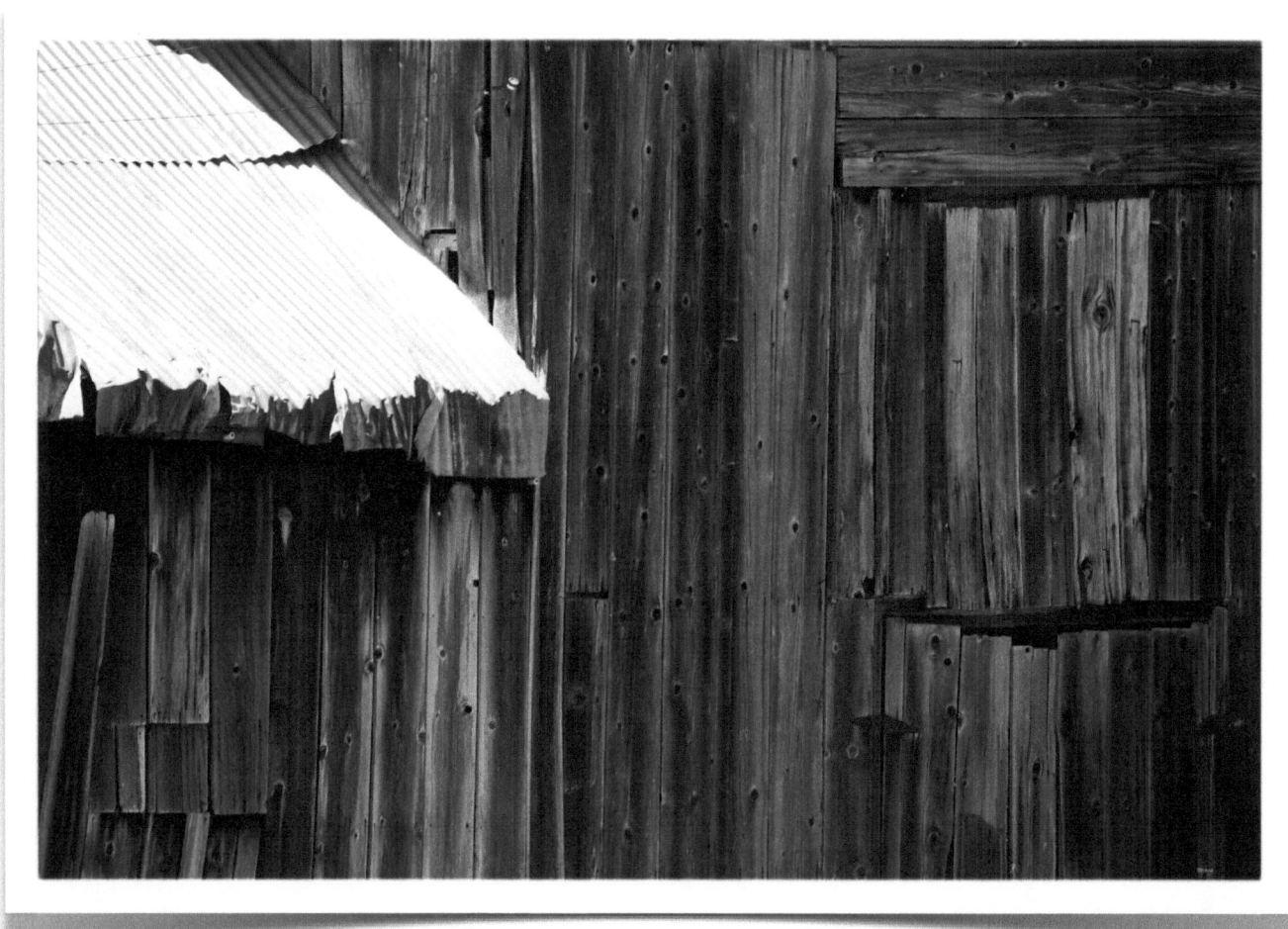

6946

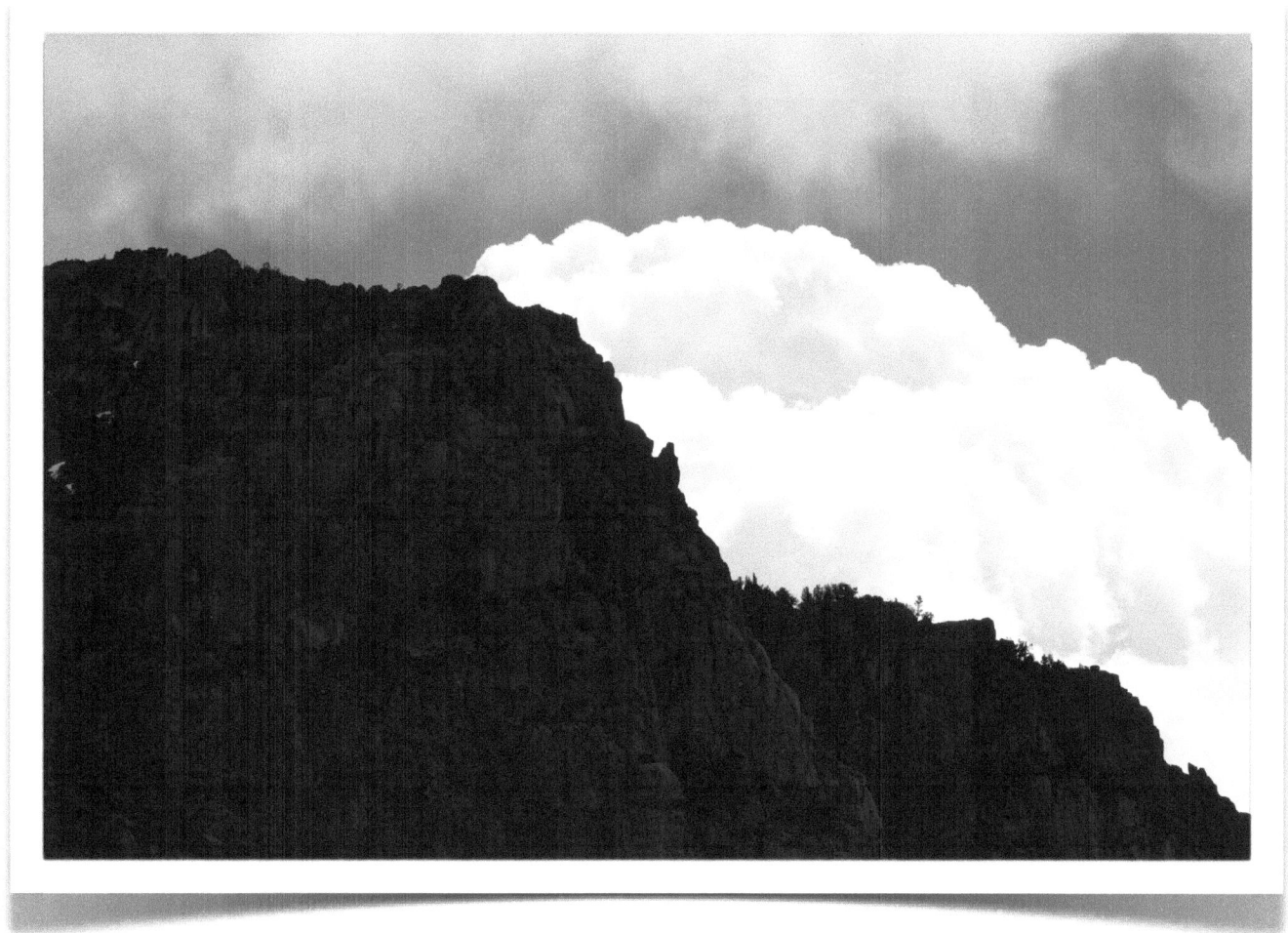

7148

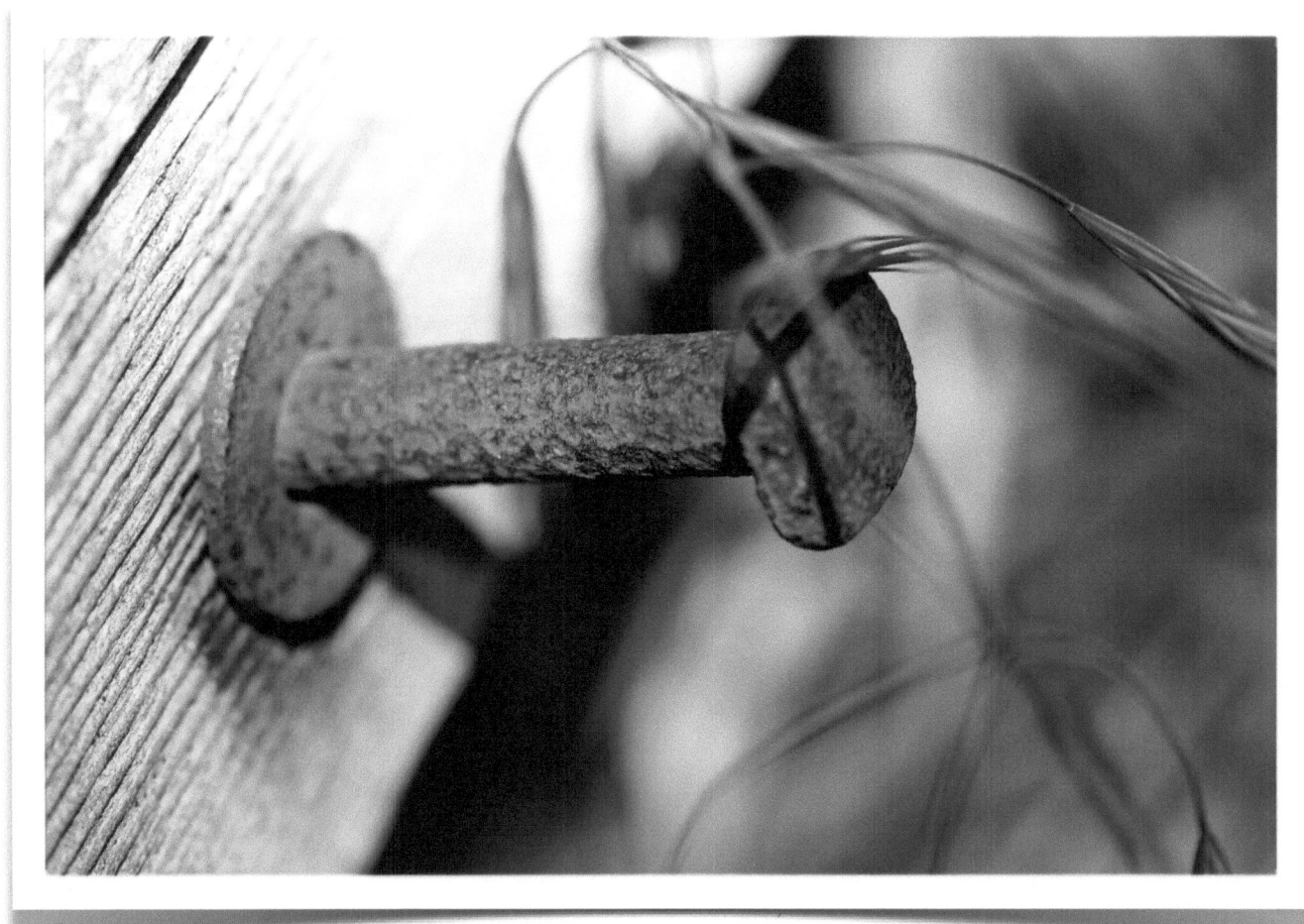

7182

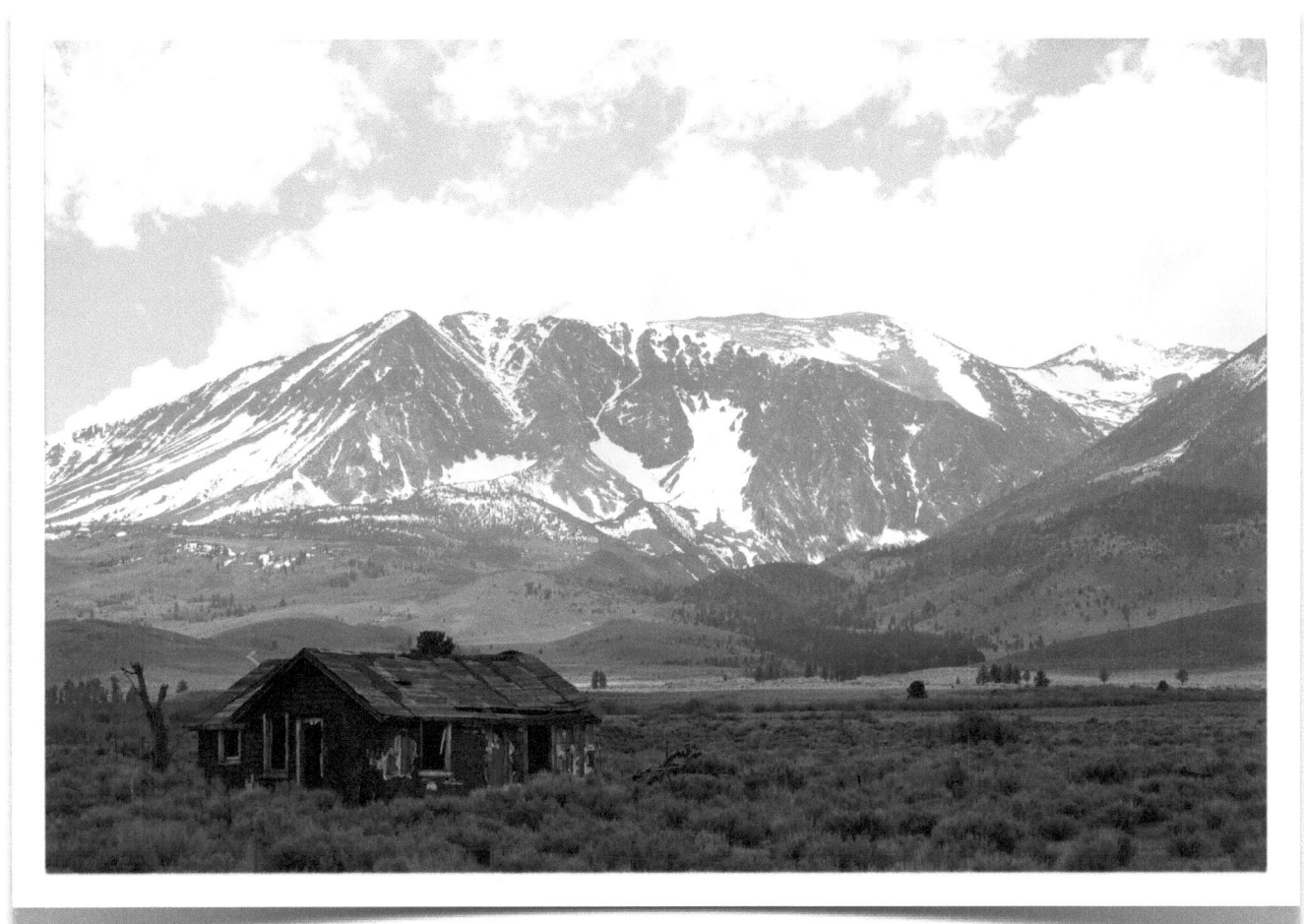

7339

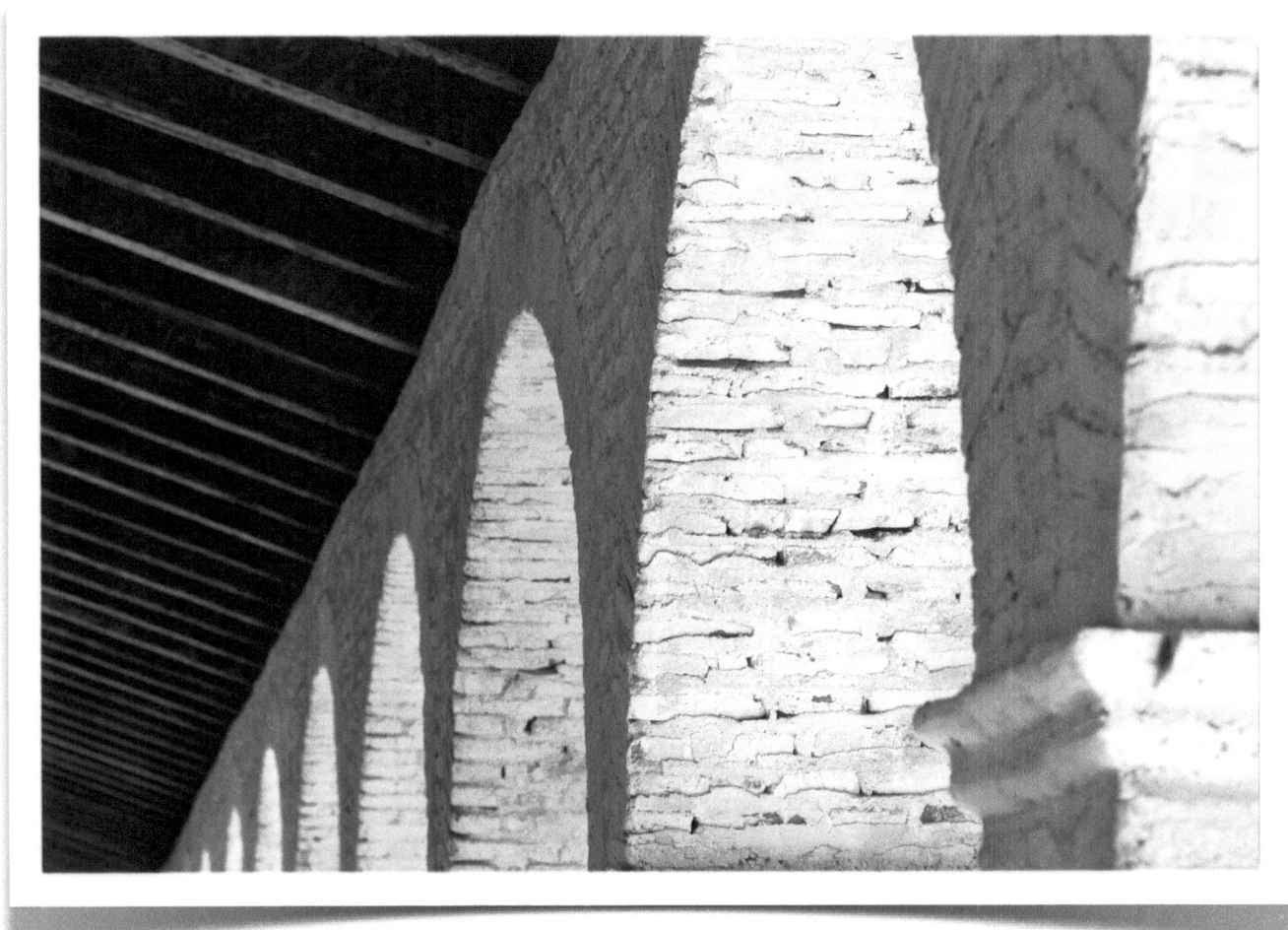

7656

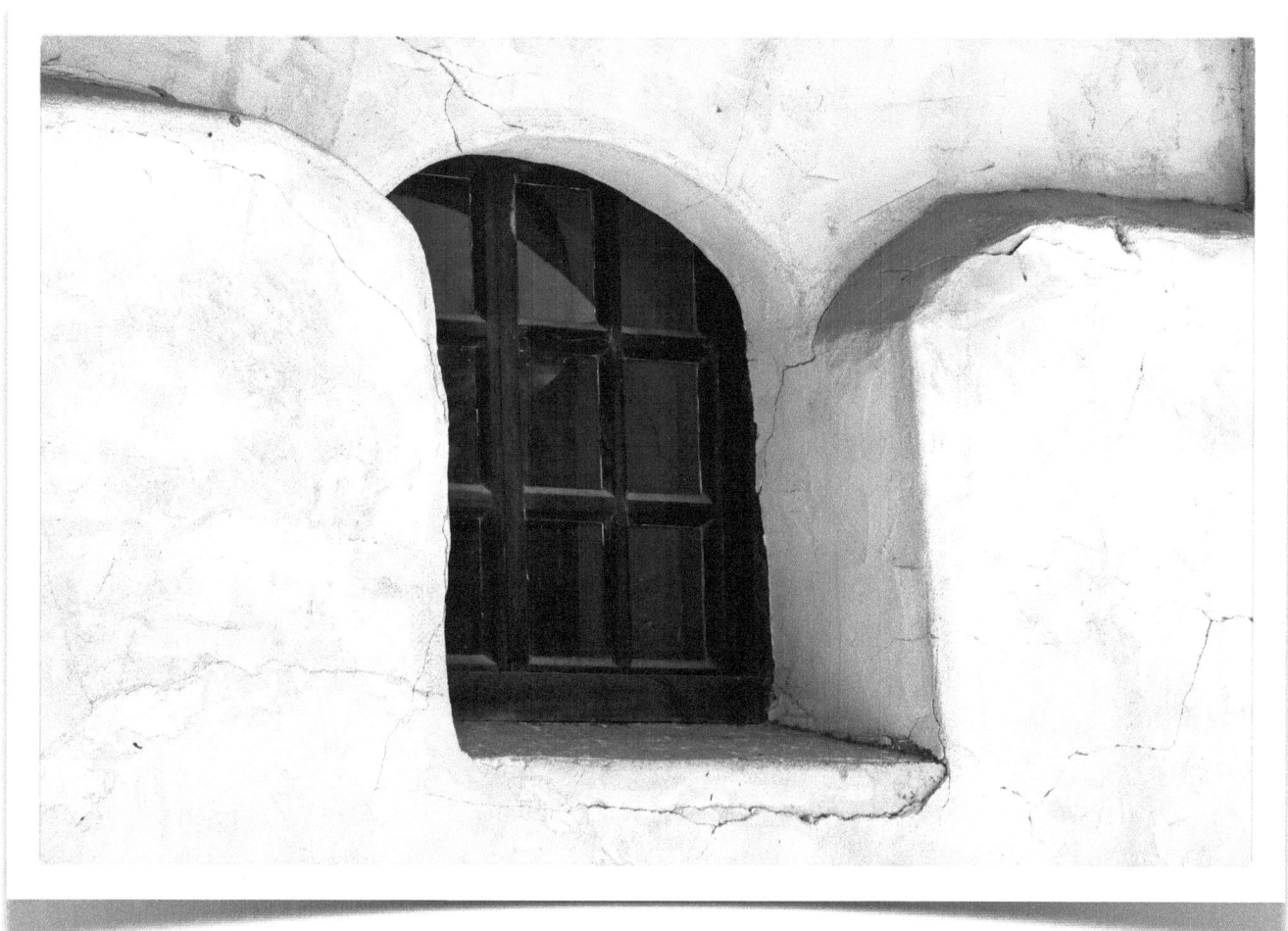

7693

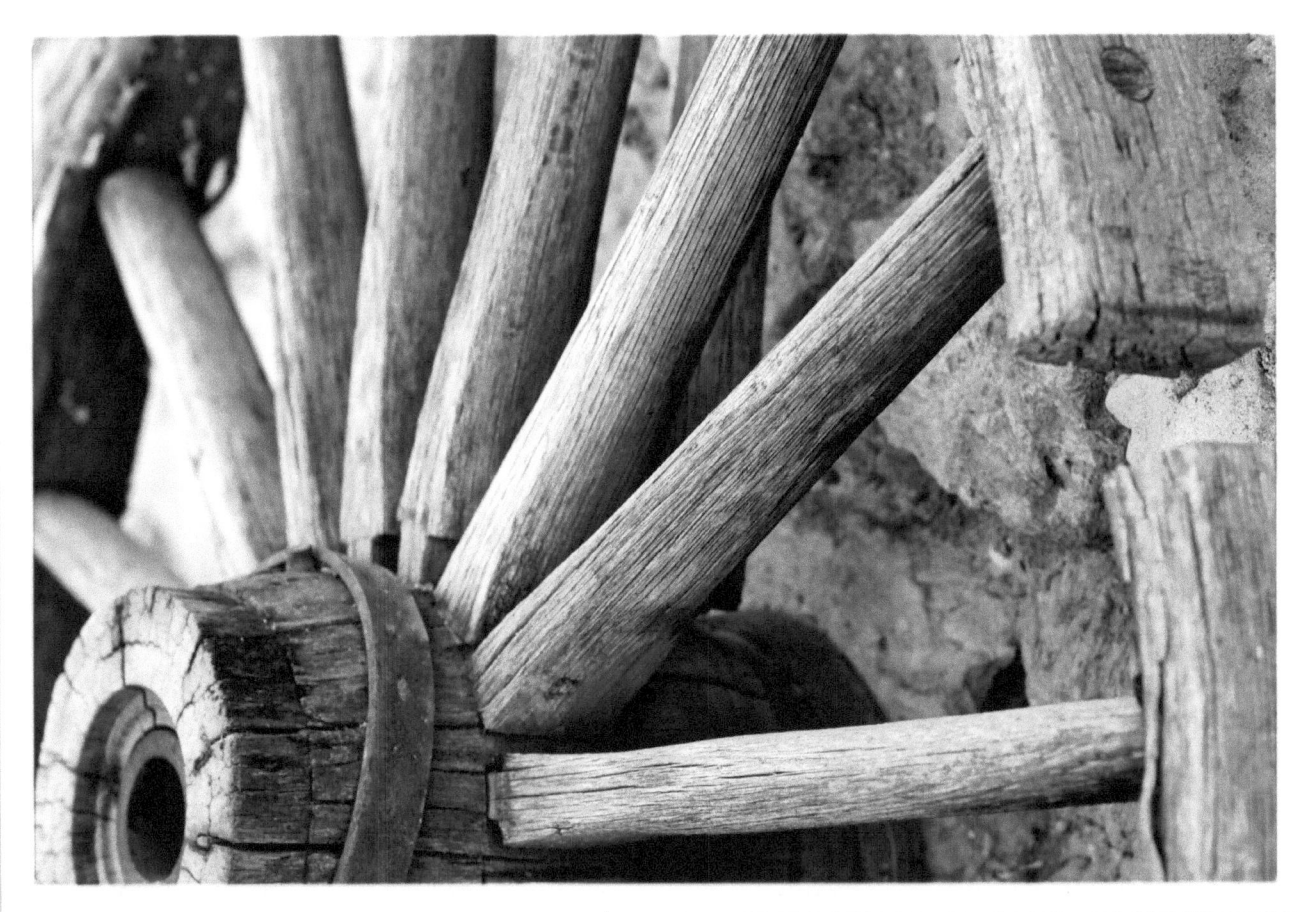

7783

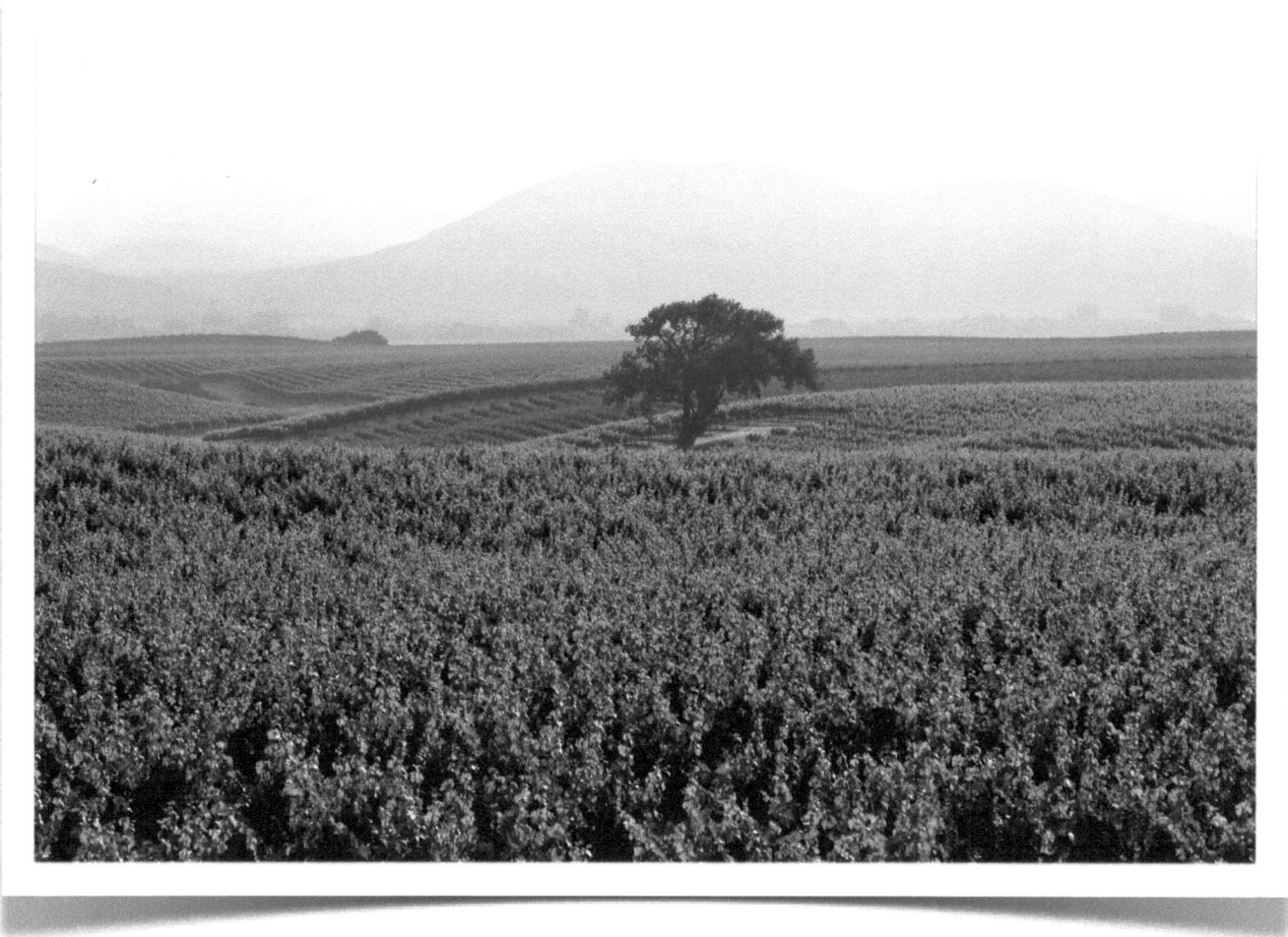

7939

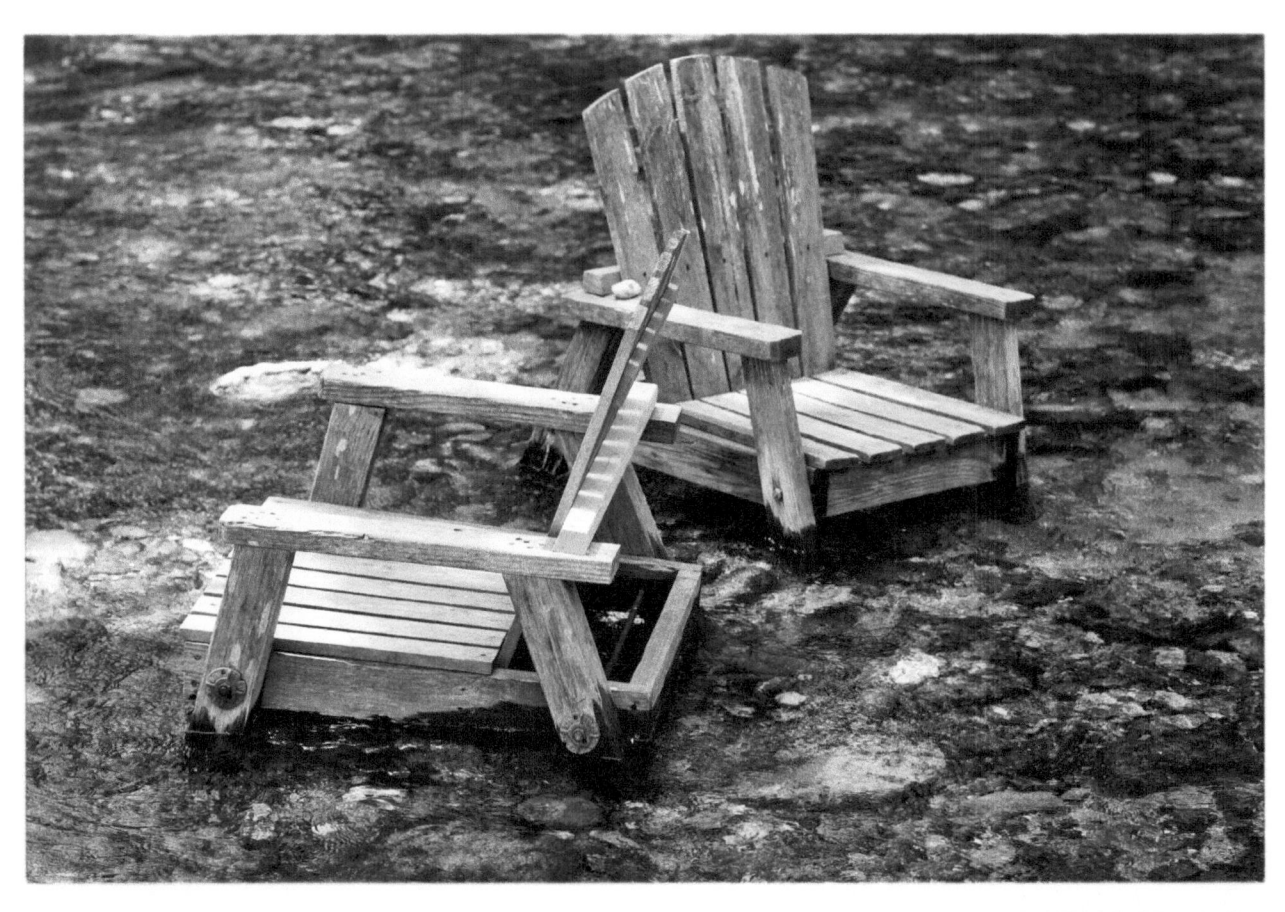

8173

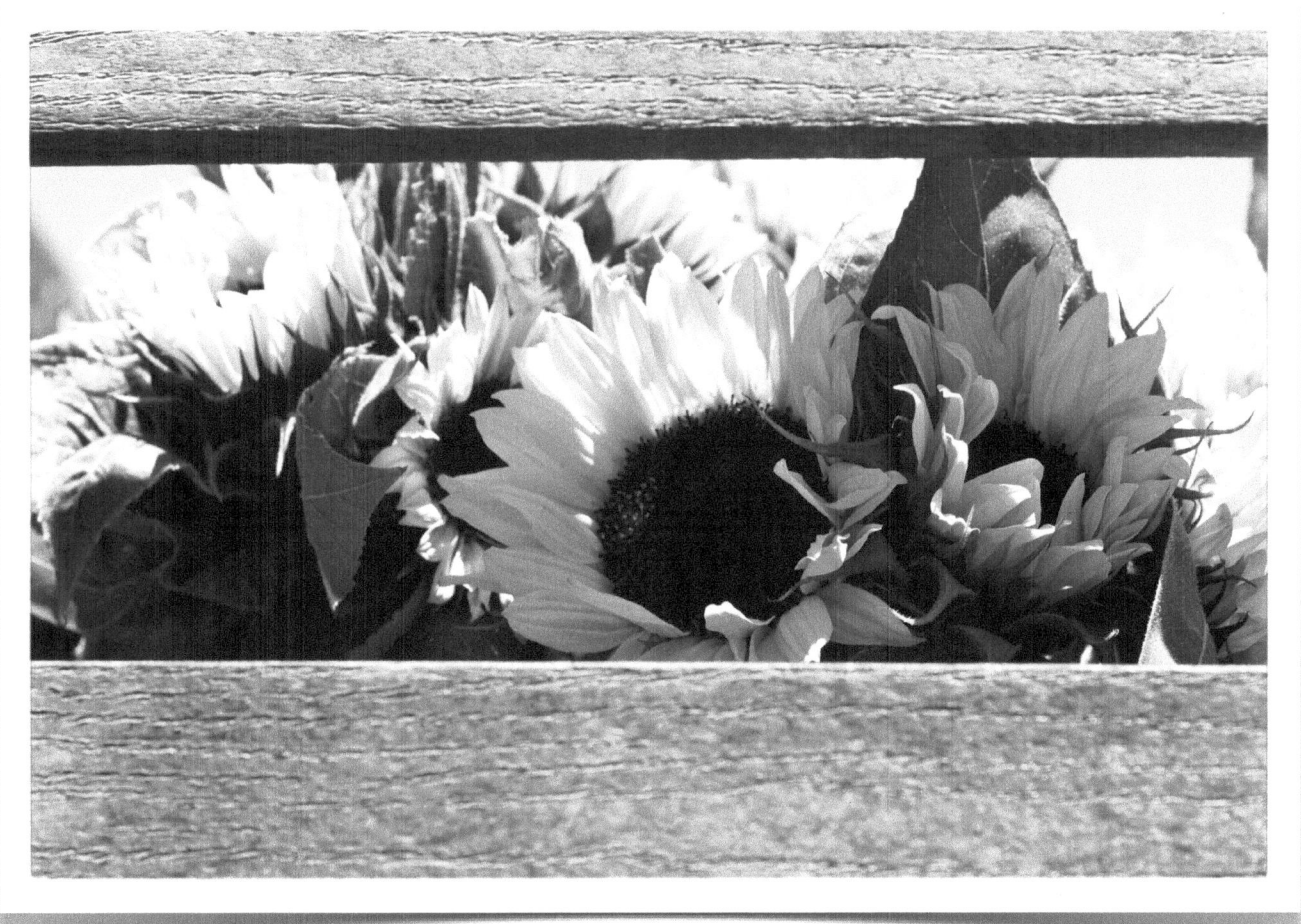

8345

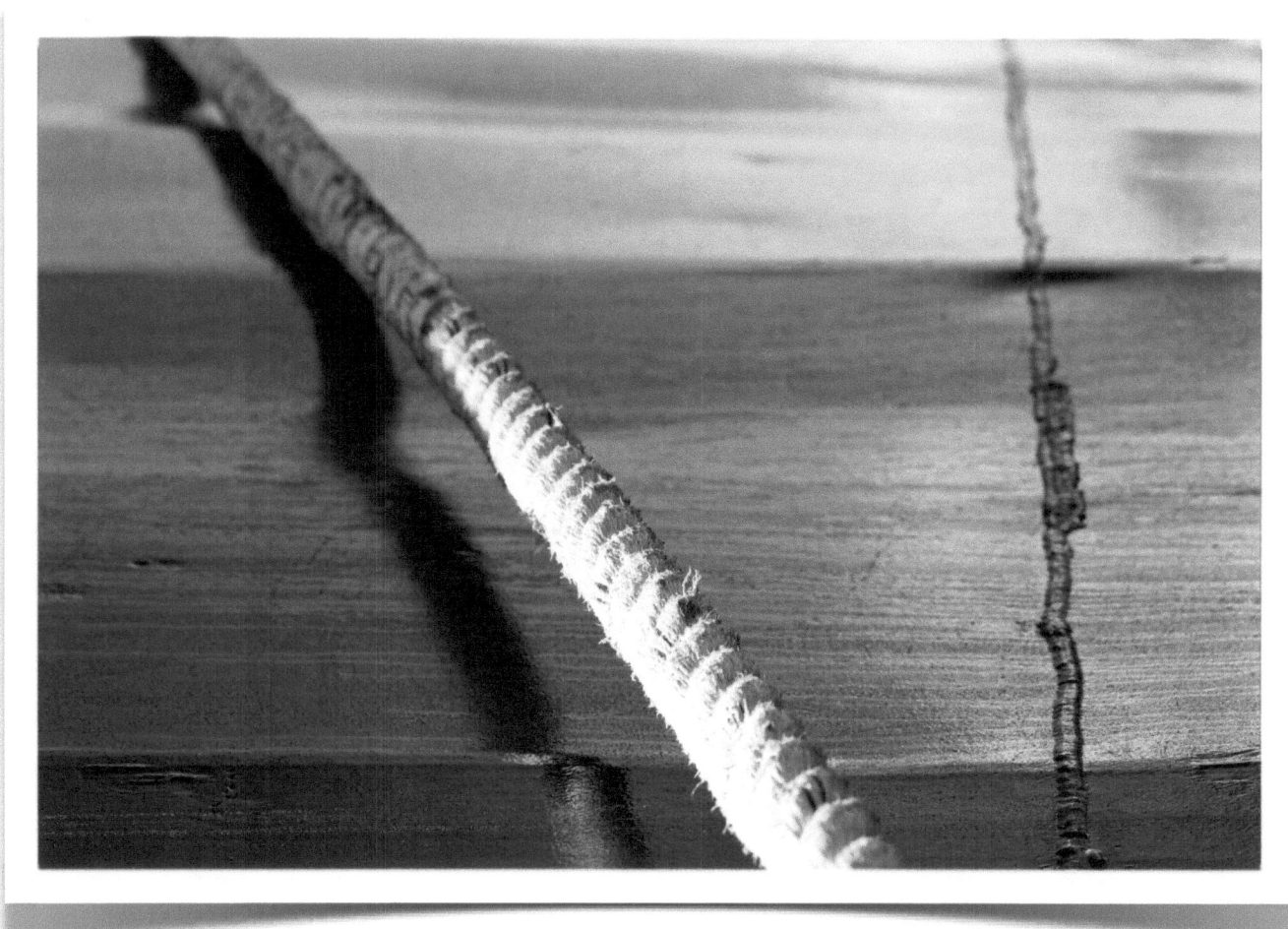

8470

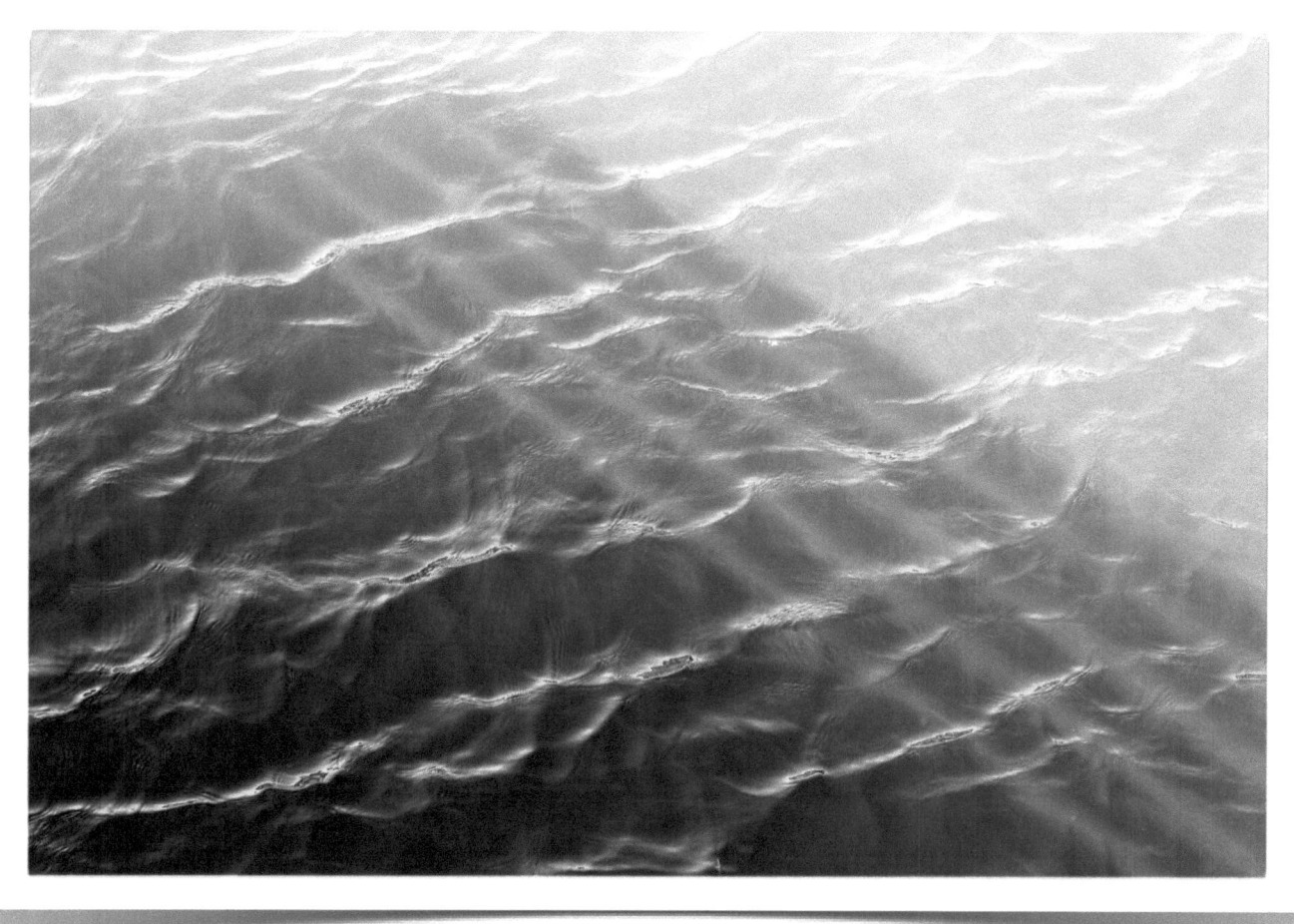

8471

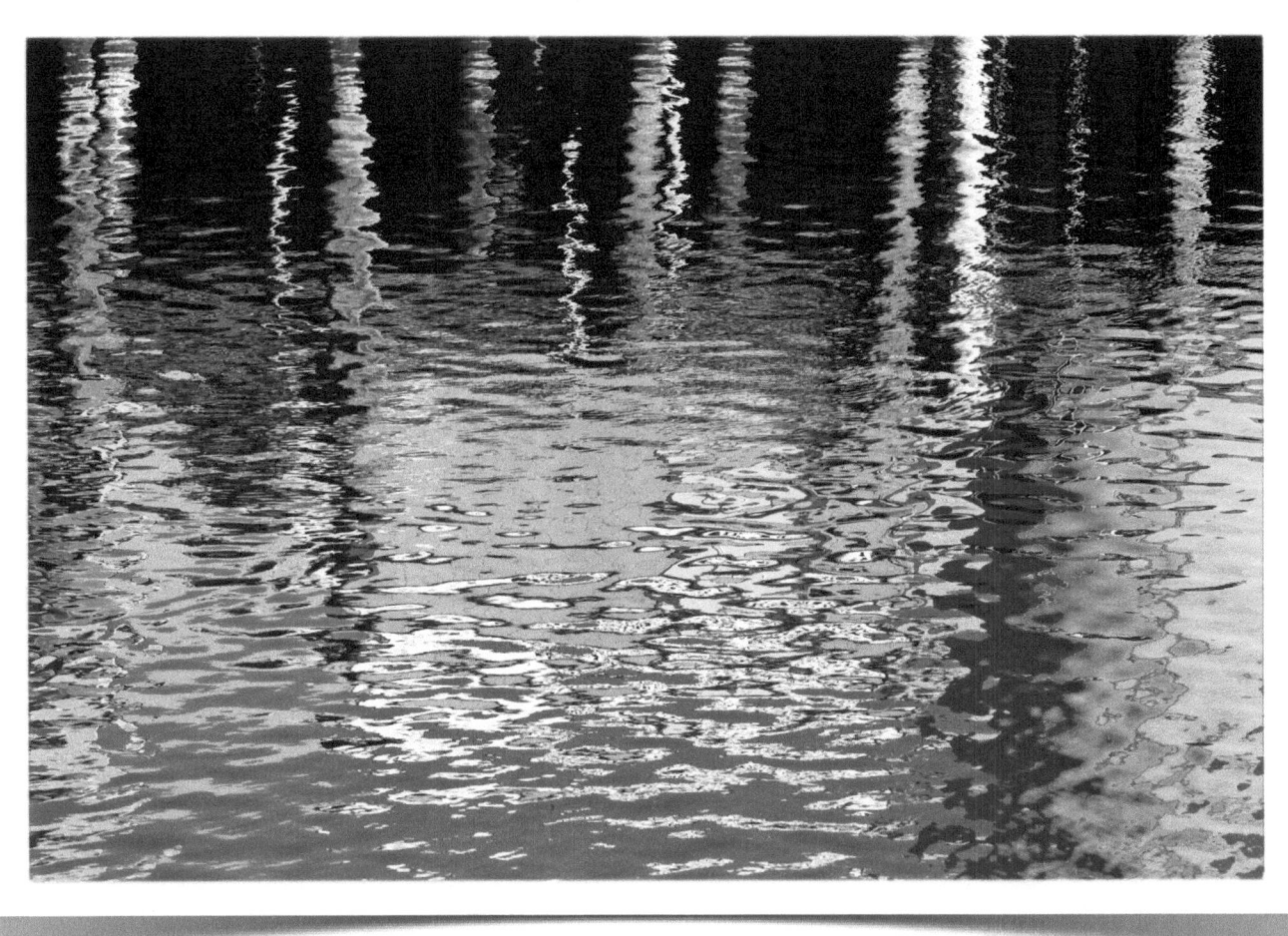

8766

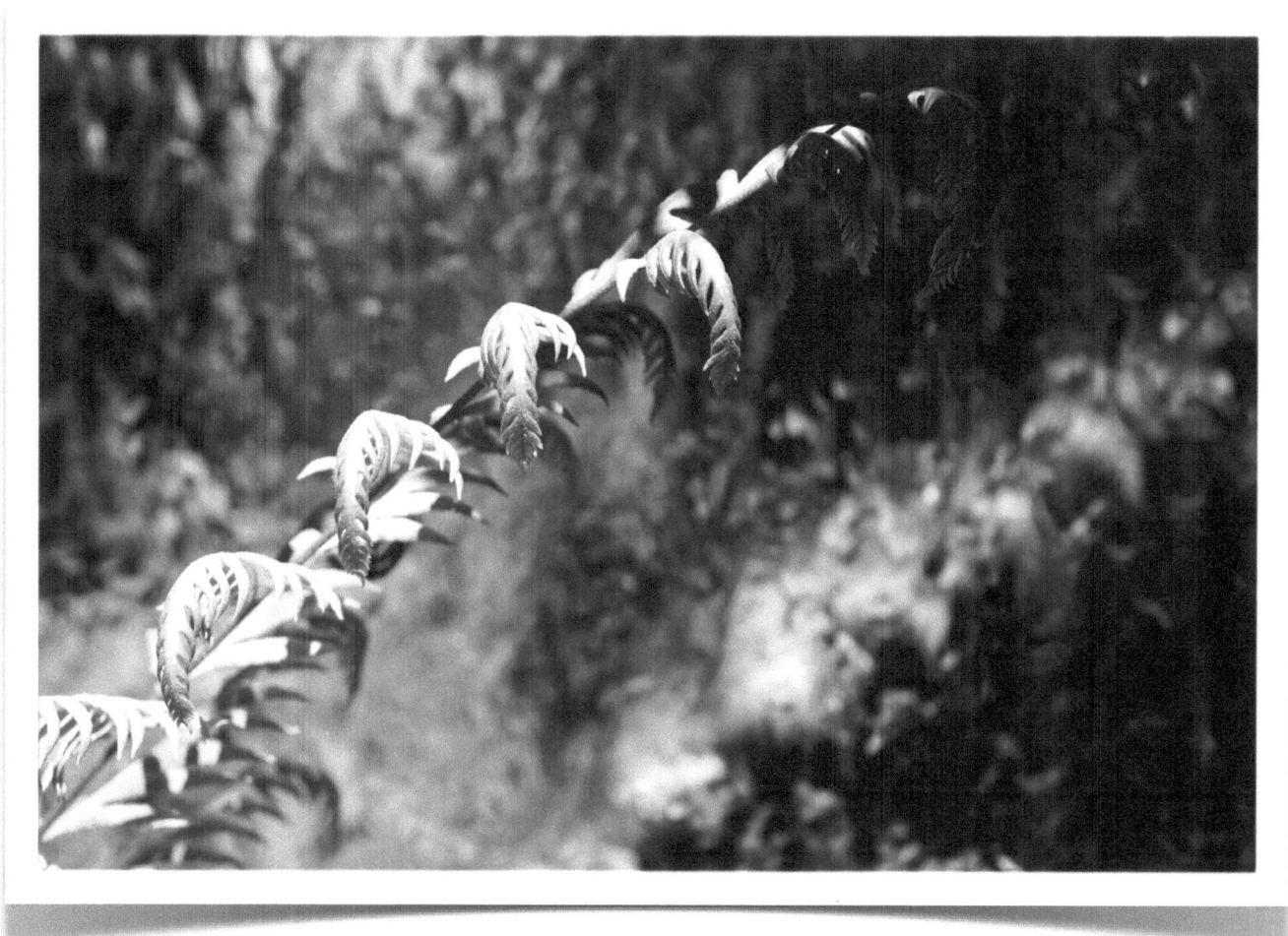

8889

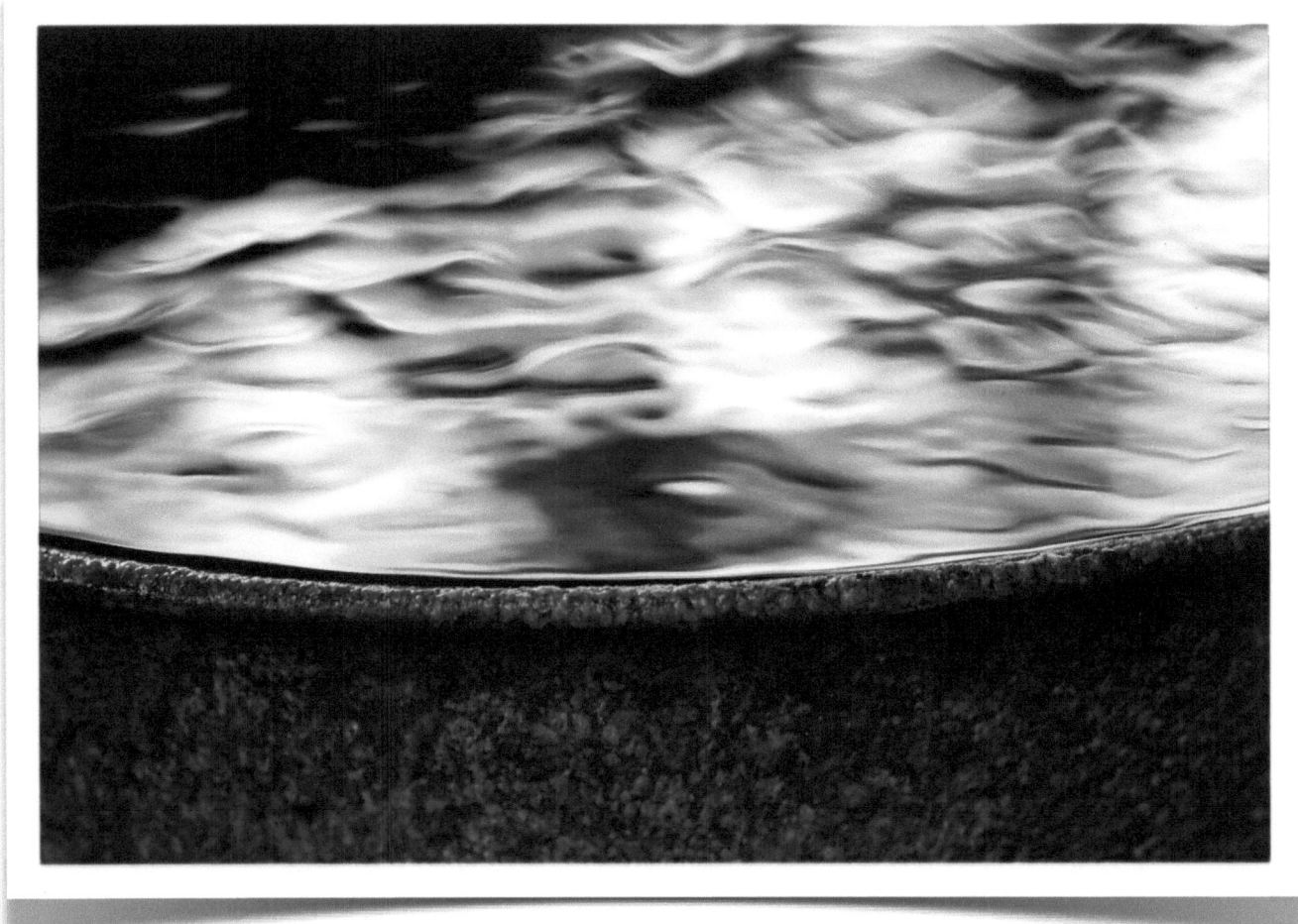

8896

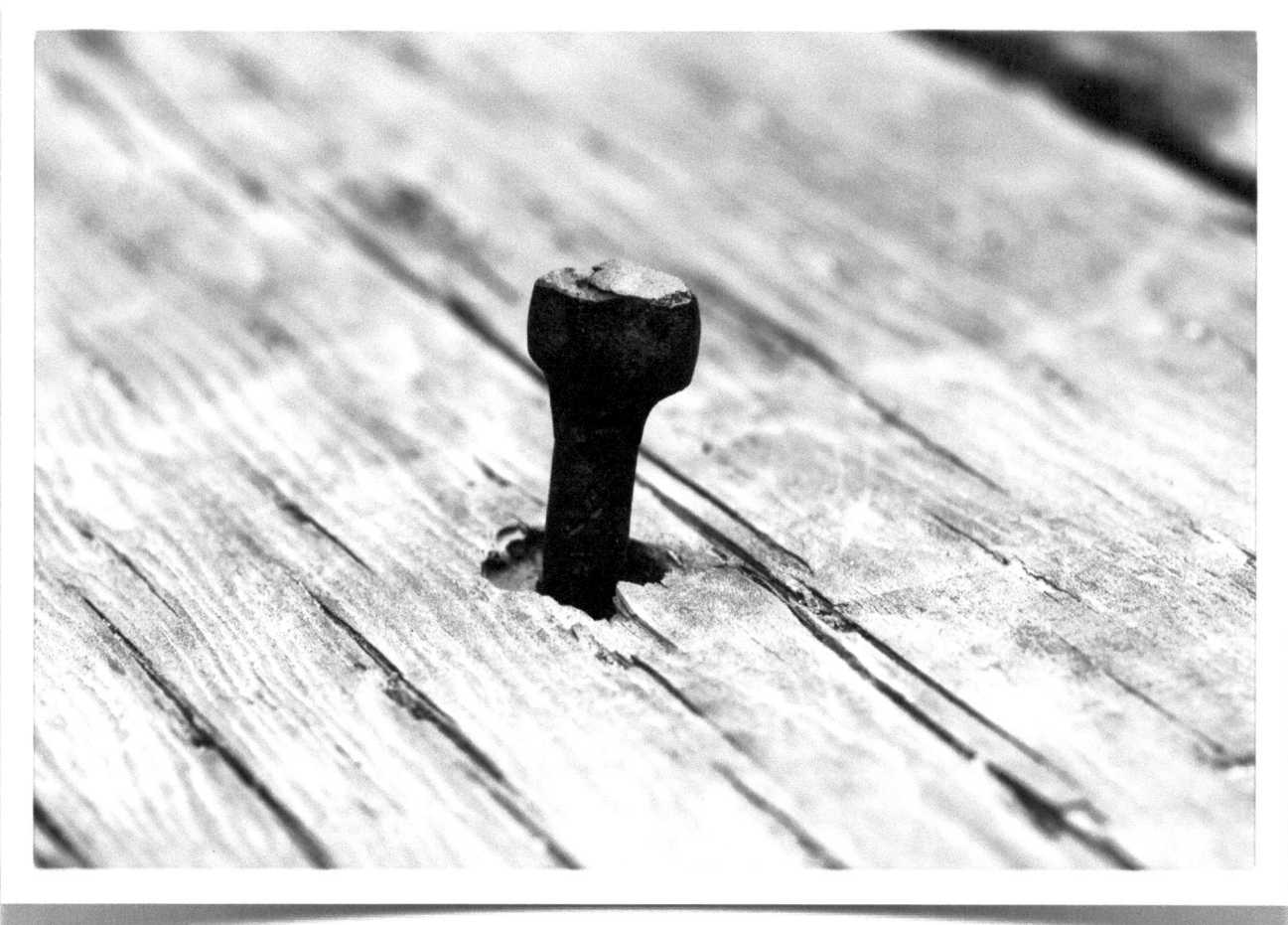

9024

9258

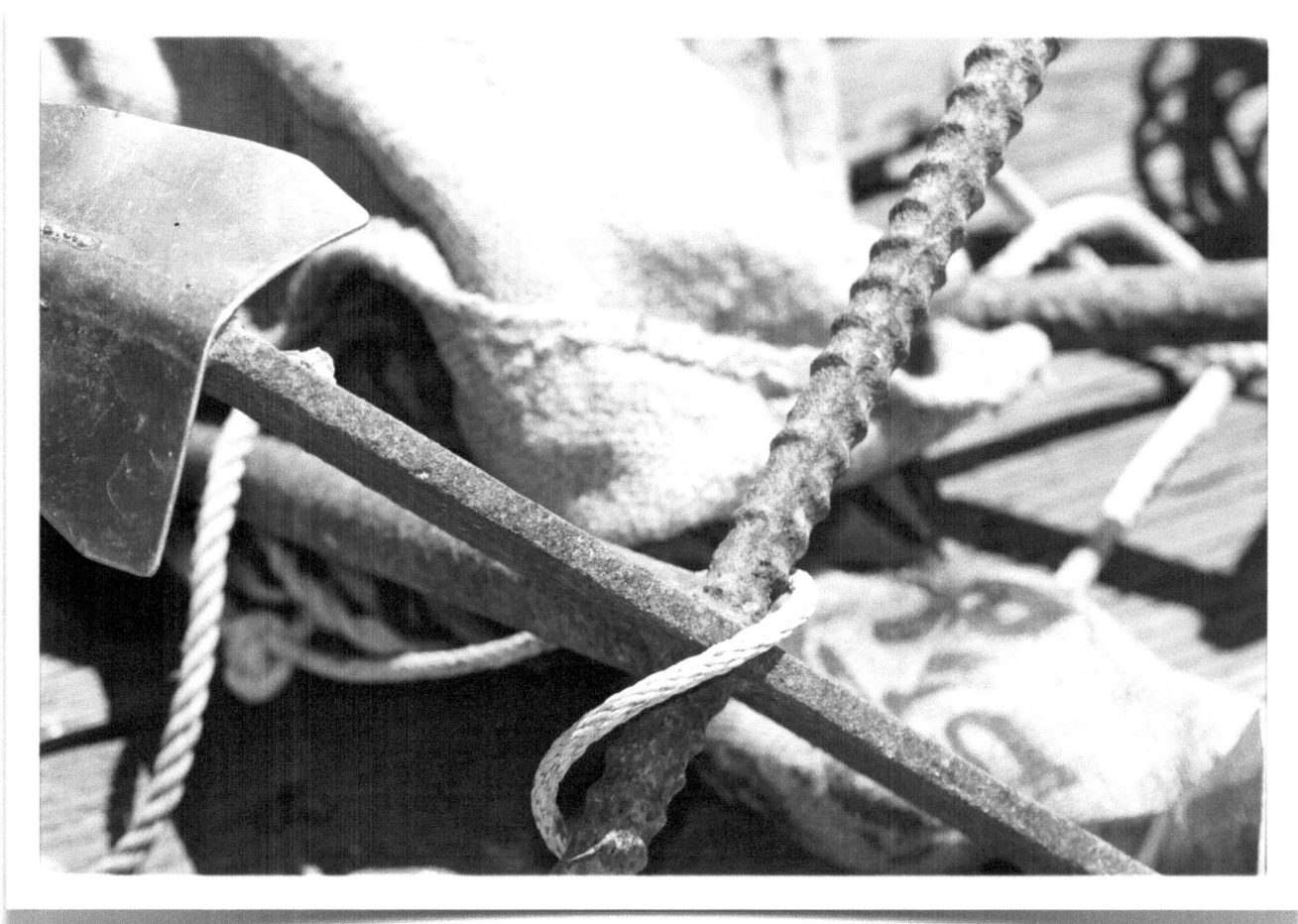

9292

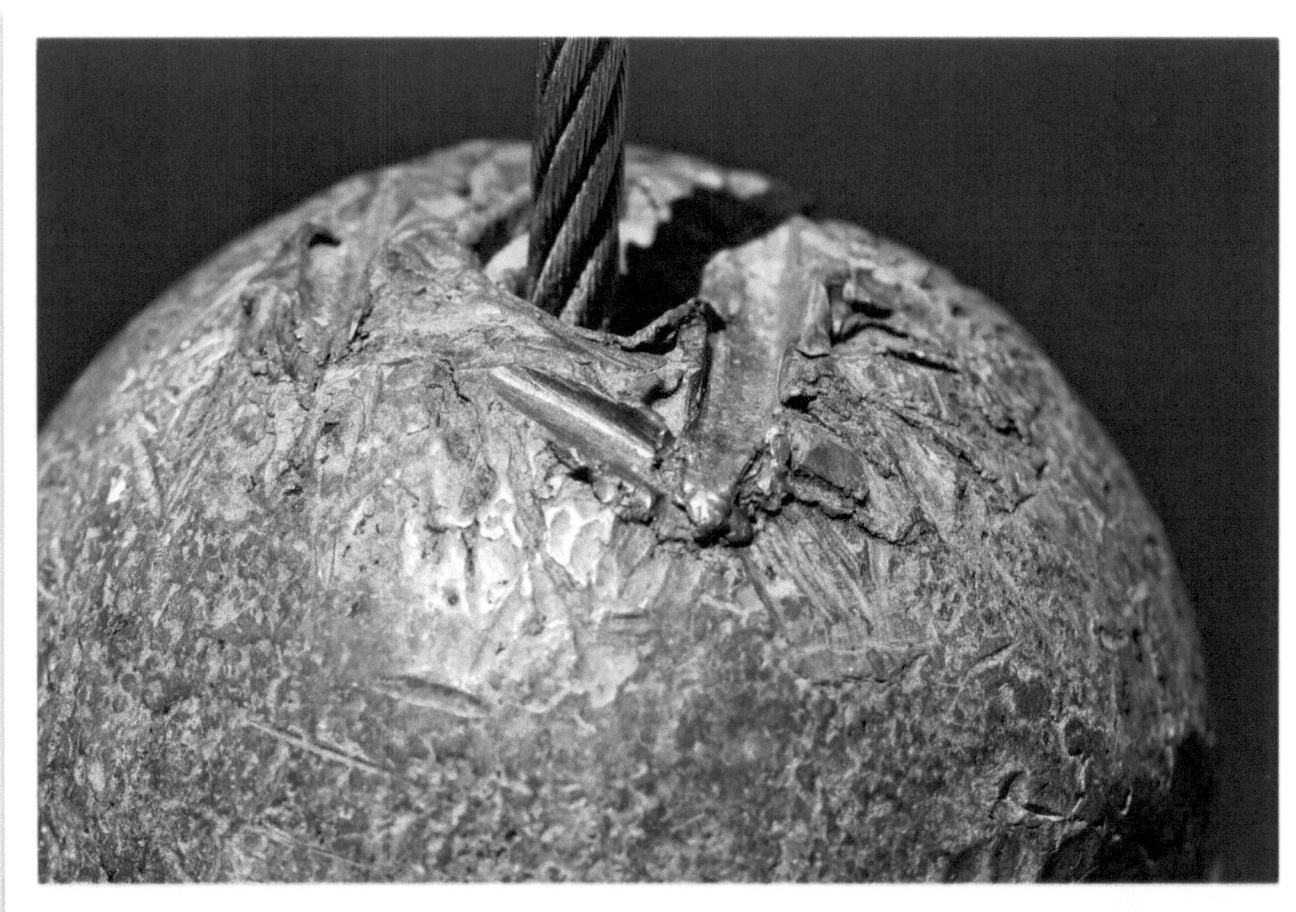

9346

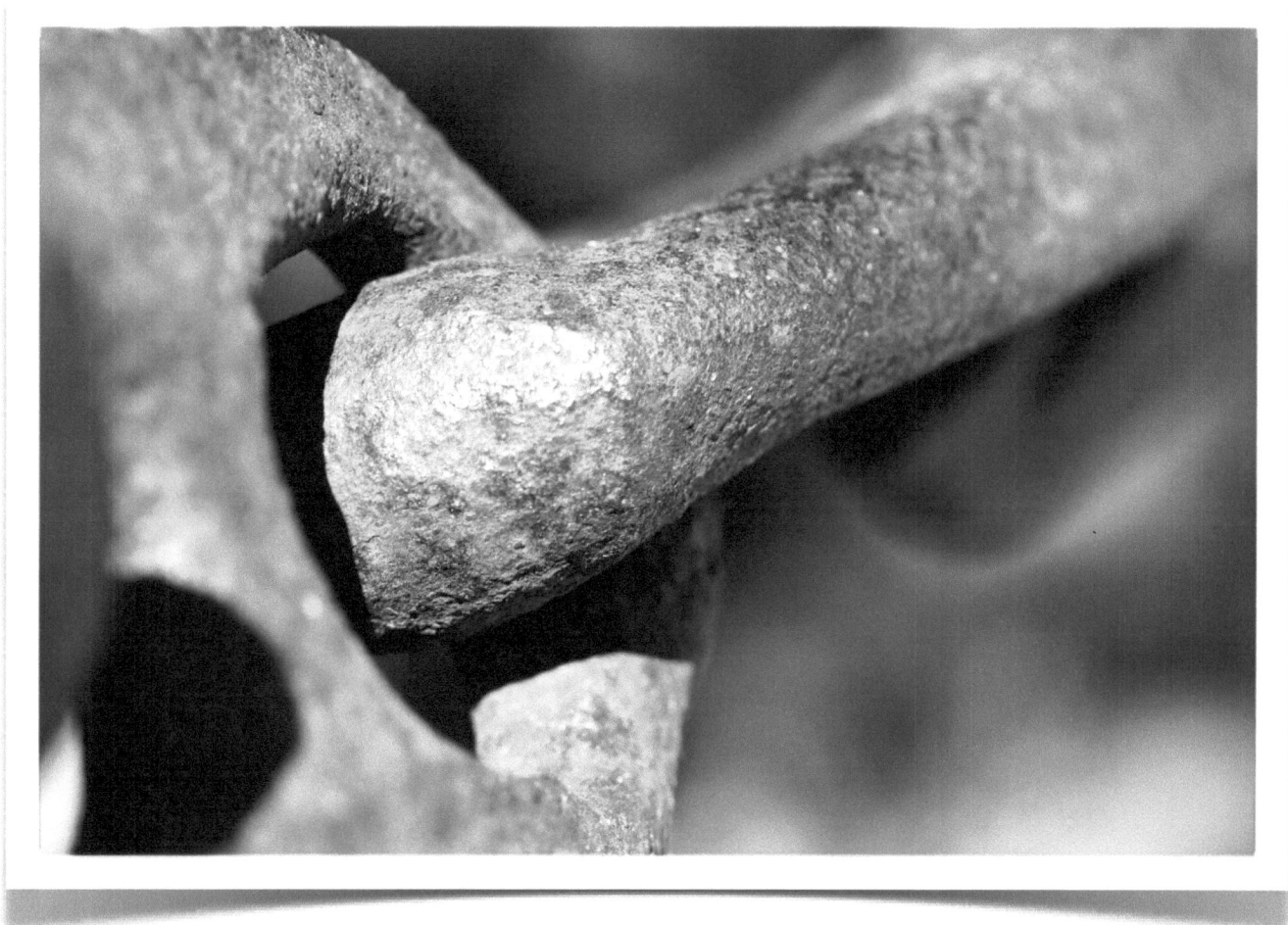

9353

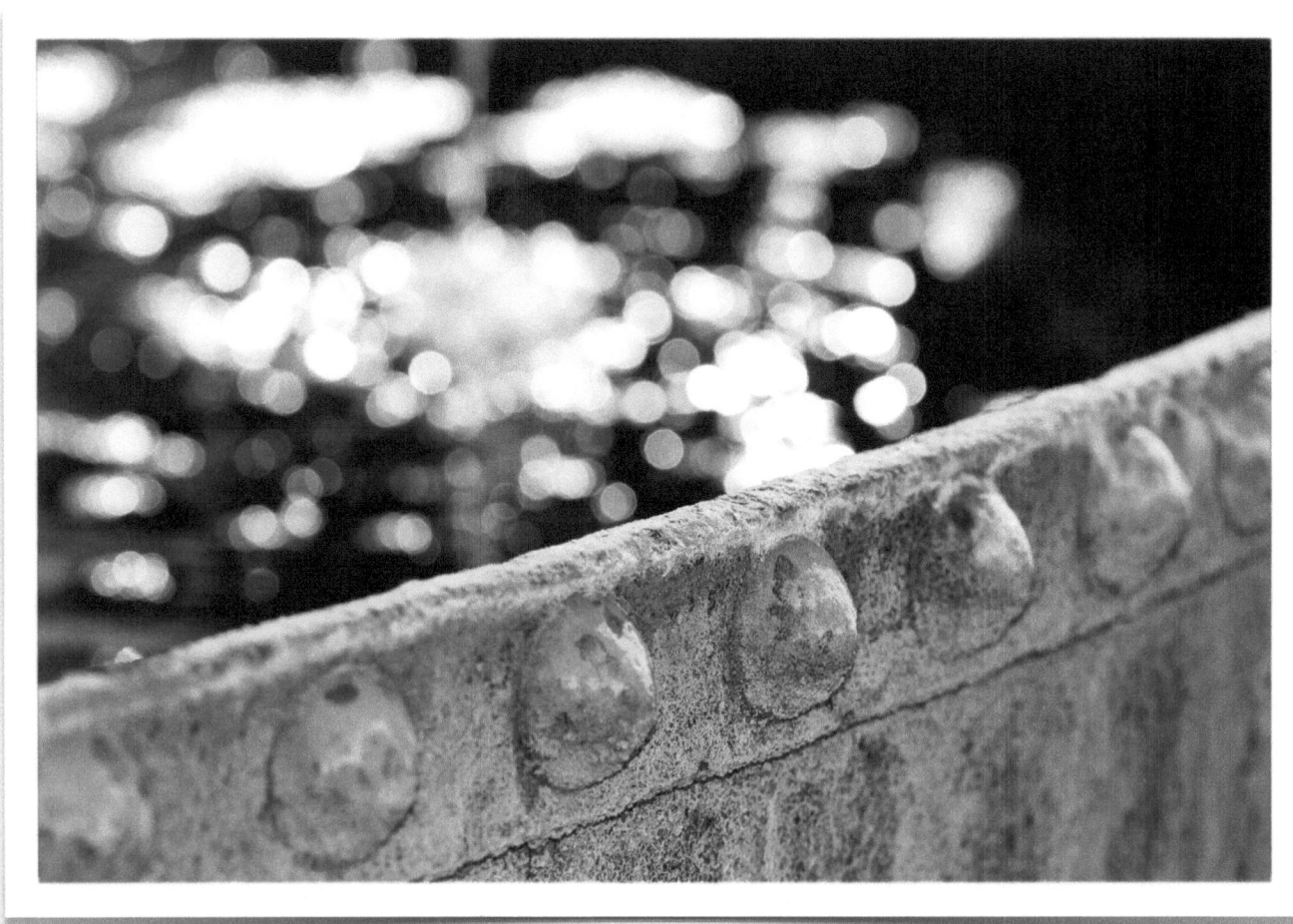

9430

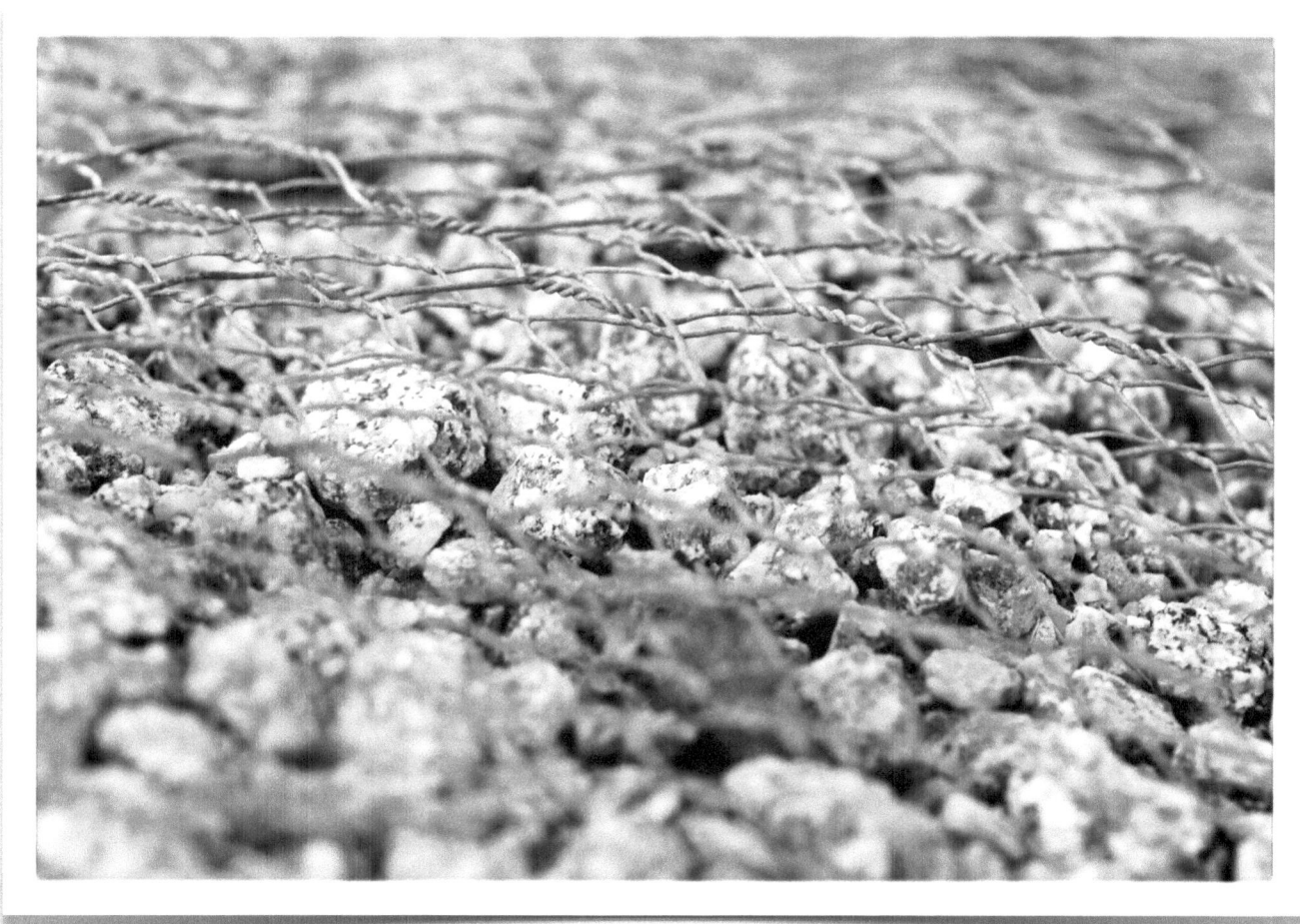

9970

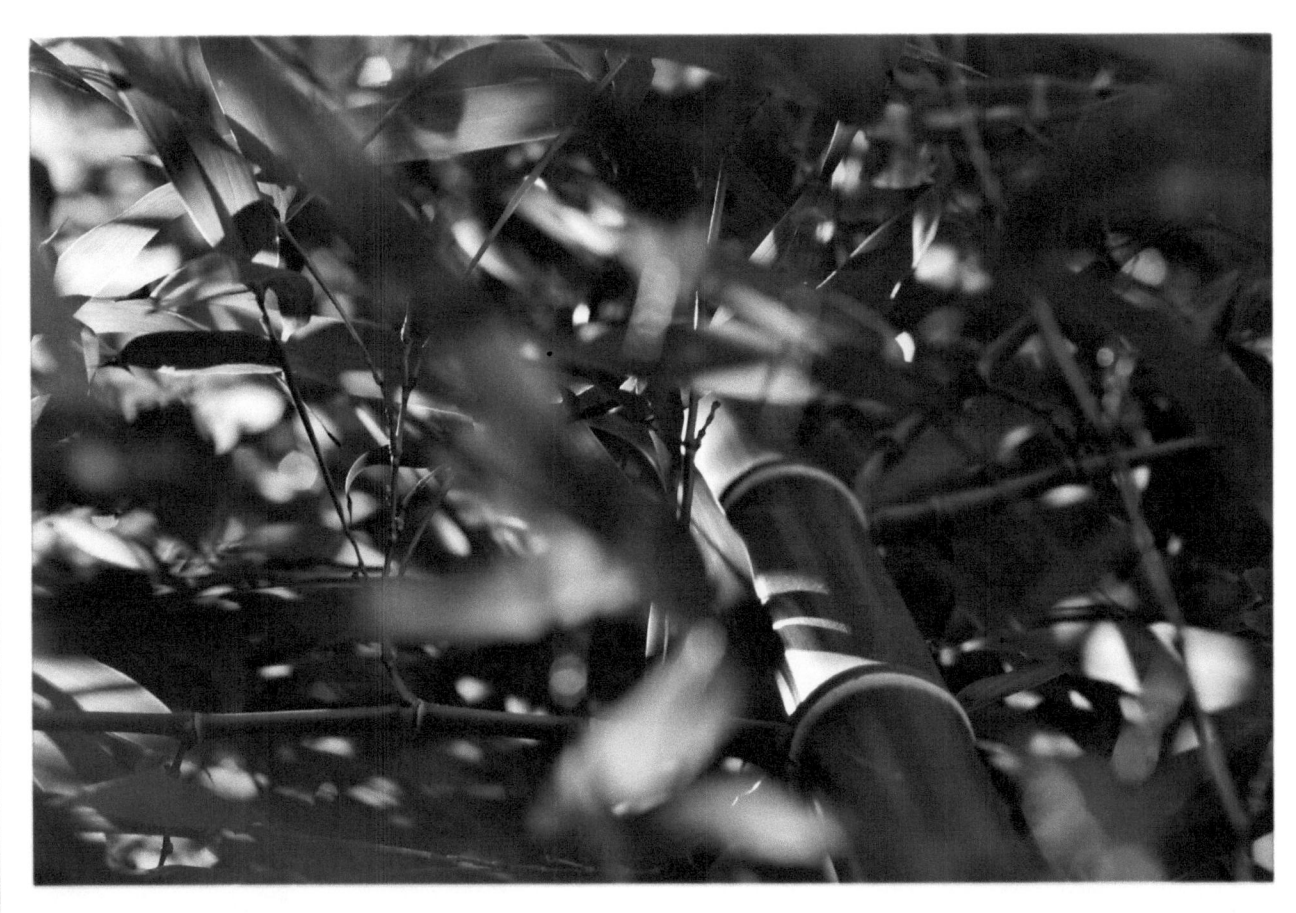

9975

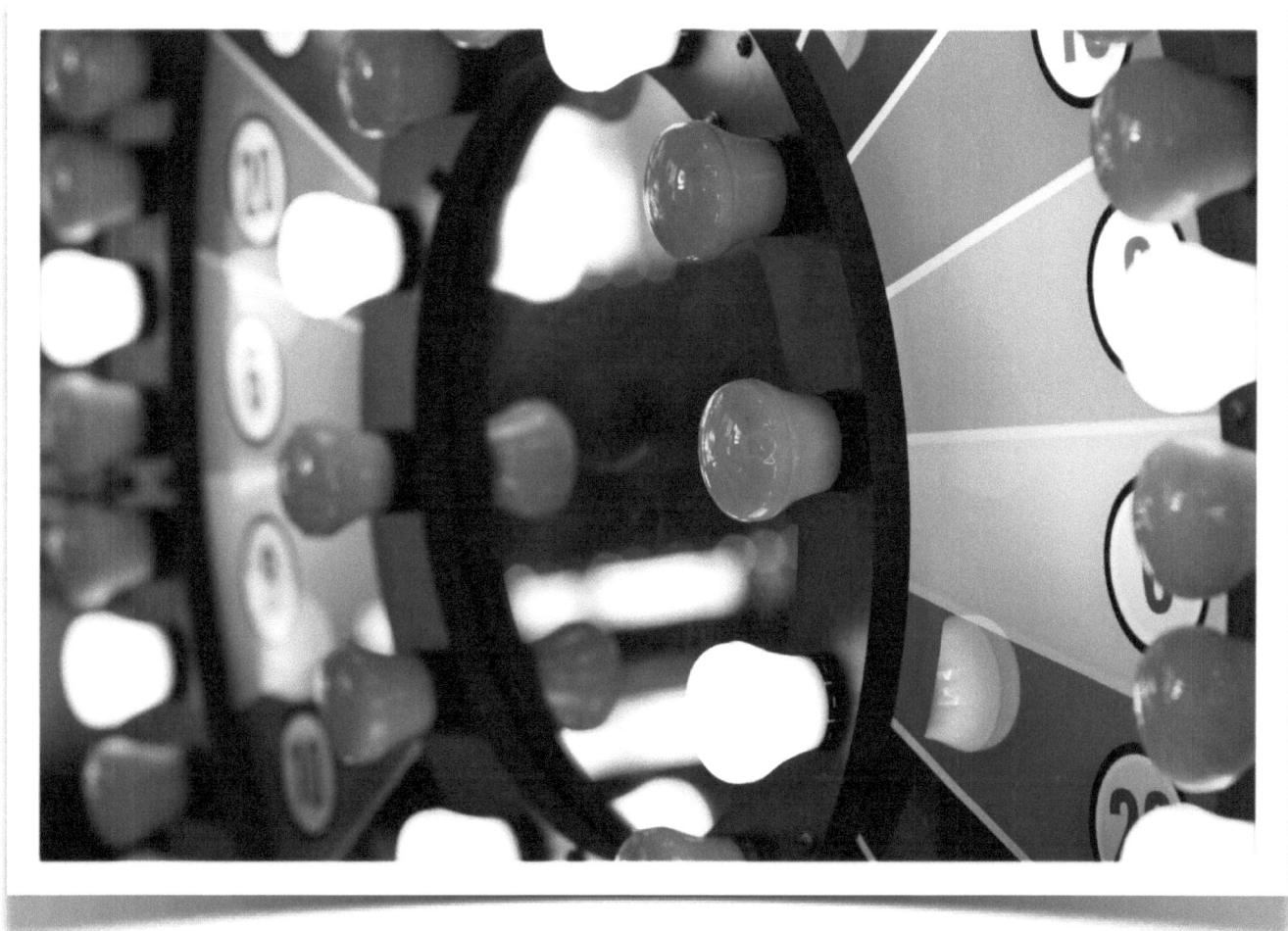

9980

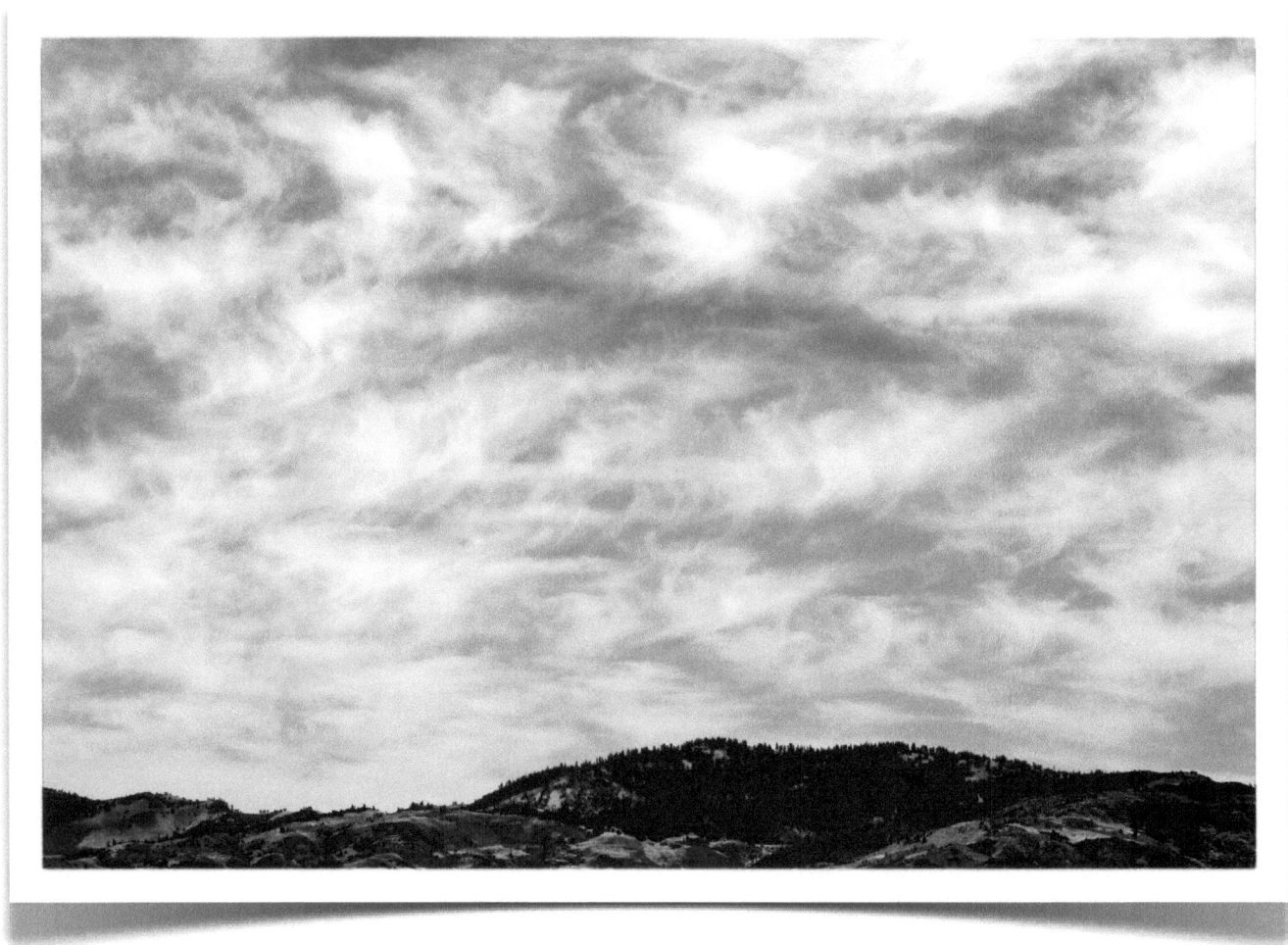

9981

9992

www.ingramcontent.com/pod-product-compliance
Lightning Source LLC
Chambersburg PA
CBHW050735180526
45159CB00003B/1234